He Sent For
WORD

Series 2

Homilies for Sundays, Year B

Fr. Emmanuel Okami

FLOREAT SYSTEMS
PUBLICATIONS
BENIN CITY

ISBN:
979-865-164-278-6

IMPRIMATUR
+ Peter Doyle
Bishop Emeritus of Northampton, UK.

NIHIL OBSTAT
Very Rev. Fr. Stephen Audu
Ilorin Diocese.
Resident at St. Peter and All Hallow's Catholic Church,
Sacramento, California, US.
Former Rector, Seminary of St. Peter the Apostle,
Eruku, Kwara State, Nigeria

*****

EDITORS
Lisa Timms
Customer Manager, Global Operations, British Airways Plc.
Our Lady of Peace Parish, Burnham, UK.

Richard Orekoya
Seminarian, Ilorin Diocese, Nigeria.

Ojochide F. Ugbaje
MayFluentials Bizhub

*****

COVER ART
Senux Media
www.senuxmedia.com

Floreat Systems
www.floreatsystems.com.ng

REFERENCES

The Holy Bible, Revised Standard Version, second Catholic Edition, Ignatian Press, San Francisco, 2006.

New International Version **(NIV)**

Holy Bible, New International Version®, NIV® Copyright ©1973, 1978, 1984, 2011 by Biblica.Inc.

Brown, Raymond Murphy; Fitzmyer Joseph A; Murphy, Roland E, eds (1990).

The New Jerome Biblical Commentary. Eaglewood Cliffs, N.J: Prentice Hall.

David Guzik's Enduring Word Bible Commentary (2018) enduringword.com

Universalis App on Android, version 1.25 (March, 2016) Universalis Publishing Limited

*****

Printed by:

Floreat Systems
Catholic Archdiocese of Benin Printing Press
30, Airport Road,
Benin City, Edo State, Nigeria
08133967455

I dedicate this book
to

the parishioners of
St. Thomas Aquinas and All Saints Parish,
Bletchley, Milton Keynes, UK.

and

Our Lady of Peace Parish,
Burnham, UK.

Foreword

In these books, *He sent Forth His Word (Years A, B, C)*, by Fr. Emmanuel Okami, we find a wealth of resource that will be of great help in the preparation for the Sunday liturgy in a Catholic Church. Catholics are well aware that whenever the Church gathers around the Eucharistic table, they enter into a mystery that is regarded as the highest possible form of prayer – the Holy Mass. In this celebration of thanksgiving, we share the Word of God in the first part of the liturgy and in the second part, we celebrate the liturgy of the Eucharist. Various components make our beautiful liturgy a vibrant, living and uplifting experience; the music ministry, the lectors who help with the proclamation of the Word, the greeters who welcome parishioners and visitors to the faith community and so on.

Deacons and priests (and sometimes where pastoral needs demand it, lay leaders or catechists), who usually lead the community at worship are required to prepare the entire liturgy. One of the most demanding processes is the teaching or preaching of a sermon. The Church takes this aspect seriously and requires the ordinary or extra ordinary minister to take it to heart. The one who preaches must prayerfully prepare, encounter the texts that are chosen for the specific Sunday of the year, and engage with the texts by consulting appropriate and trustworthy Catholic sources and commentaries.

The scriptures chosen for each Sunday are connected; from the Old Testament, the Psalms, the epistles from the New Testament and the third and last reading, from the Gospels. The minister should be able to lucidly show the relationship between the texts, intelligently pass on the message and relate it to contemporary and people's daily lived experience. Without wasting time on unnecessary performances or entertainment, the minister must present the Good News to the people of God exactly for what it is; the GOOD NEWS of and about Jesus Christ!

In this book, Fr. Okami presents a resource to help us, priests and people, as we all prepare in our homes for the best and most fulfilling spiritual experience at the liturgy. I find Fr. Okami's method simple and thematic. He presents each Sunday's message clearly enunciated and well organised. This book will be a treasure trove for preachers, because it is not pedantic or cumbersome. It is sometimes scholarly, but not to the extent of becoming redundant to non-specialists. There is even a good dose of humour to make the experience light, without losing its seriousness.

There are quite a good number of published books on preparing Sunday reflections, however, you find some are often too heavily couched in theological language and some are too wordy and unnecessarily long. I find Fr. Okami's reflections apt, intelligent, educative, spiritual and very much in line with our Catholic tradition. As I congratulate Fr. Okami, I also heartily recommend this book for people in ministry, for catechists and teachers of the faith, for small basic Christian communities, for Bible studies and even for private times for Lectio Divina.

May the Lord bless His words in our minds and by them, lead us all to everlasting life.

Fr. John Segun Odeyemi, Ph.D
Parochial Vicar, St. Paul's Cathedral Grouping.
Diocese of Pittsburgh, Pennsylvania, USA.

*****

Author's Note

I am immensely grateful to God for the grace to realise this onerous project. It is a project I started in 2016, when I received the inspiration to do this. It has pleased God in His wise providence that this work be completed this significant year.

This year the Church marks the 1,600th anniversary of the death of St. Jerome, the Patron Saint for biblical scholars. This year is also the tenth anniversary of the release of the rich and spectacular Post Synodal Apostolic Exhortation *Verbum Domini,* a document on the importance and relevance of the Word of God in our modern world. So, it is God's phenomenal plan that this humble work, which began four years ago, be completed at this time.

He Sent Forth His Word is a seven book series of homilies for Sundays (Years A, B, C), Weekdays (Cycle I and II), Liturgical seasons (Advent, Christmas, Lent and Easter), and Feasts and Solemnities.

I want the reader to take note that some of the homilies were written and delivered in Africa (Nigeria) and some were written and delivered in Europe (England), and so this dynamism comes to play when reading these reflections. I have also tried to intentionally re-work some of the homilies to have a more universal countenance. In any case, no matter the original context and diverse cultural experiences, the Word of God still speaks to everyone in varied ways.

I do not presume that everyone will agree with all the contents of these reflections; not even the Holy Bible can claim such universal acceptance. However, what I pray and hope for is that these homilies will be of benefit to someone seeking to understand the Word of God and grow in faith. I also pray that this humble work may help preachers and teachers of the faith in their ministry of teaching.

My special thanks to all the Bishops who reviewed these books and offered vital and helpful suggestions. I am indebted to all those who edited these works; it has passed across the table of many editors, but that is not to claim that it is flawless. My aim is not to write a flawless book, but to share with others the fruits of my meditation and the riches of God's Holy Word.

Many thanks to all who supported these publications in one way or another. If God wills it, this will be the beginning of many more to come.

May the revelation of the Word of God bring us light and understanding and lead us to Jesus who is the Word made Flesh, the Truth, the Way and the Life.

Fr. Emmanuel Okami
A Priest of Ilorin Diocese, Nigeria,
On Mission in Northampton Diocese, UK.
Word of Life Ministry (WOLM), Milton Keynes, UK,

Reviews

The book, *He Sent Forth His Word*, by Rev. Fr. Emmanuel Okami, is a very practical, down to earth explanation of the Sunday readings. It is a treasure of short messages of hope, in simple language that moves the heart. This is a text that readers can apply to their daily lives. Priests and the lay faithful will find it very useful in their quest to increase their faith in the Word made flesh.

+ Augustine O. Akubeze
Archbishop of Benin City
President of Catholic Bishops' Conference of Nigeria

*****

In his outstanding homilies in this book, *He Sent Forth His Word*, Fr. Emmanuel Okami has brought the scriptures home to the reader. They are well expounded with a refreshing newness of life. The style is simple and clear and makes for easy reading, and the very rich scholarly output, which is well delineated, is very enlightening. Its didactic explanatory and very appropriate imageries, with current human experiences, make for ready assimilation of the lessons therein. The practical true to life deductions from the scripture readings are inspired and inspire one into action for a better Christian life. Each reflection carries a powerful persuasive tone, with emphasis on putting Christ's teaching into practice. What a priceless handbook of daily meditation for all!

+ Michael Patrick Olatunji Fagun
Bishop Emeritus of Ekiti, Nigeria.

*****

Bringing God's Word to people in a clear and distinct language is a unique gift. Fr. Emmanuel Okami through this book, *He sent forth His Word*, has not only explained the Word of God but has made it practicable in the life of everyone who comes in contact with this book. Fr. Okami, in interpreting the text, did not limit himself to the English meaning but went to the source, the Greek and Hebrew words and gave a detailed interpretation of the text. This is a well-written book, and I recommend it for everyone who truly wants to grow in his or her daily Spiritual journey. It is a complete guide in understanding the readings in the Catholic Church and the writer has offered a deep connection between the readings of the day.

Most Rev. Francis Obafemi Adesina
Catholic Bishop of Ijebu-Ode Diocese

*****

What Fr. Emmanuel Okami sets out to do in each one of the homilies in *He Sent Forth His Word* is to engage the reader in a conversation, as well as a reflection on the Word that is Life, the Word that gives Life, and the Word that is the Lamp for our feet and the Light for our path. What he has succeeded in doing is to produce a well-articulated publication that speaks to the enquiring mind, and to those seeking knowledge and understanding. It is put together in simple plain language, easy to follow and devoid of the complexities of scholarly "biblical language." The homilies are short, crisp and conversational, with real time stories of personal encounters and anecdotes.

Like the two travellers on the road to Emmaus whose hearts were afire with Jesus' recounting and explanation of the events foretold by the Prophets, (Luke 24:13-35), the reader can receive fresh inspiration and illumination and gain new perspectives along the milestones signposted by these homilies, which I thoroughly recommend to all Christians who desire to grow in understanding of the Word. I particularly recommend them to priests, deacons and lay leaders who often need to consult such a collection of homilies in the course of preparing their own.

Rev. Fr. George Ehusani
Executive Director, Lux Terra Leadership Foundation

*****

Fr. Emmanuel gives a clear reflection on each Sunday's readings, which help us to get to the heart of their message. His direct approach and clear teaching enable us to understand the message, reflect on its impact on us and consider how to respond to it personally.

Fr. Simon Penhalagan
Northampton Diocese, UK.

*****

This book of Fr. Emmanuel Okami's homilies is spiritual guidance to live a Christian life in this modern world. All the homilies are very simple to follow, yet rich and deep, full of messages of God's love for us. I love the homily on "God delights in Mercy".

This book is the work of the Holy Spirit in Fr. Emmanuel's life and waits to enrich everyone with these gifts. I would highly recommend it.

Anitha Babu
Software Developer, Research and Development , Sage UK Ltd
Parishioner of Our Lady of Peace parish, Burnham, UK.

Faith is the beginning of the spiritual journey. Once the believer comes to faith, we need virtue to establish the moral direction of our lives, and unless that direction is established, what we do will be of little consequence. This collection of homilies, *He Sent Forth His Word* by Fr. Emmanuel Okami, delves into the world of the believer through the avenue of the Scriptures, speaking words that will help foster virtue.

In addition, these homilies are intended to inspire the faithful towards becoming proactive members of the body of Christ, active participants of the Holy Eucharist, empowered by the Holy Spirit for a life of service. I recommend this book to every churchgoer in search of helpful spiritual guidance towards adding virtue to faith.

Rev. Fr. Dr. Anthony Mario Ozele
Catholic World Evangelical Outreach. Nigeria.

*****

He Sent Forth His Word
Series 2

Homilies for Sundays, Year B

Table of Contents

*****

Second Sunday In Ordinary Time

CALLED TO BE WITNESSES FOR CHRIST

READING TEXTS:
1 SAMUEL 3:3b-10, 19; PSALM 40:2, 4, 7-10;
1 CORINTHIANS 6:13-15, 17-20,
JOHN 1:35-42

T oday is the Second Sunday in Ordinary Time, year B. I shall be preaching on what I have titled: *Called to witness to Christ.*

Let us begin the reflection from the readings of today. The First Reading of today tells us about the call of Samuel. The Lord called Samuel three times; Samuel eventually responded, and the Lord set him aside as a great prophet in Israel.

The nucleus of the reading is that God called Samuel to be His mouthpiece, His witness, the conscience of the society, and Samuel responded.

The response of today's Psalm is a response to a divine call: *see I have come to do your will.*

In the Second Reading, we see St. Paul exercising his ministry as one called and chosen to be a teacher of truth. He reminds the Christians in Corinth that by their call as people of God, they must avoid every conduct and way of living that is sinful. Here, he was particular about adultery.

In today's Gospel, we see a cascade of this call and response. John was called to make Christ known to the world, and this he did. John witnessed to Christ, and among those who profited from his witness was Andrew. We see Andrew witnessing to his brother, Peter, who will in turn witness to the Jewish nation.

Just like Samuel in today's First Reading, the Lord has called us as believers (2 Peter 1:10). Called to do what? Let me just mention 5 things:

- To be the salt and light of the earth.
- To serve the Lord in various capacities.
- To a life of holiness.
- To work out our salvation while on earth.
- To witness to Jesus in this world.

Let us reflect on this fifth point.

How are we to witness to Jesus in our societies? Often, we hear that we are called to witness to Jesus, and the question in our minds is: How?

Today, I shall be preaching on four ways to witness to Jesus.

I. *Talk to someone about Jesus:*

We should share our knowledge of the faith with someone. We should not be shy in talking to someone about the Christian faith, about Jesus, or heaven. We should start up a discussion about salvation, about grace, about God's mercy.

2

There are three messages of hope that the world needs to hear today:

- There is hope for them in Christ Jesus.
- God loves them as they are.
- That there is a heaven and there is a hell.

II. *Live a good, disciplined and upright life:*

This is what St. Paul charged the Corinthians to do; a good Christian life. An upright, disciplined, good moral life is a life of witness; a life that preaches. The kind that St. Peter talks about in 1 Peter 2:12. A Christian who curses, insults, revenges, engages in malice, betrays, gets drunk, is immodest in words and deeds, is involved in wickedness of any sort, or bears false witness - what kind of witness is someone who does this? This is more a problem of identity crisis.

III. *By reaching out to people:*

This entails us reaching out to the poor, the needy, the helpless, the aged, those at the margins of the society, those the world scorns. Like Jesus, we must stretch out our hands to touch the 'social and spiritual" lepers among us. These acts of kindness to those who can't repay us, are always an act of a valid and fruitful witness to Jesus.

IV. *Courage to be different:*

When everyone is choosing the path that offends our Christian faith and conscience, we should try as much as we can to be different from others. We witness to Jesus when we say, "I cannot; I will never, it is against my faith. I will not join you, count me out." (to those things that are incongruent with our received faith). This courage is lacking in most Christians today. We have more cowards than valiant. Many of us place more value on our lives than our salvation; such will eventually lose salvation in the bid to protect their lives.

Let us not be shy, afraid, timid, so respectful, or so calculative that we can't reject what violates our conscience, no matter the threat or the consequence of whoever is behind the agenda.
(Matthew 10: 37-39).

There is no way we can gain heaven without being ready to face fire, and it is in facing fire here on earth with courage and faithfulness to God, that we avoid an eternity in the fire in the next life (Revelation 12:11).

Happy Sunday and God bless you.

*****

THE LORD IS CALLING YOU

READING TEXTS:
JONAH 3:1-5, 10; PSALM 25:4-9;
1 CORINTHIANS 7:29-31;
MARK 1:14-20

Today is the Third Sunday in Ordinary Time, year B. Our reflection is titled: *The Lord is calling you*.

The First reading tells us about the message of God through the Prophet Jonah to the Ninevites. Nineveh was such a massive city of the Gentile world, the capital of Assyria. At several times they conquered and colonised Judah, looted and destroyed the temple and carried able-bodied men to exile. It was populated by heathens, a centre of godlessness and yet it was so prosperous.

Their prosperity amidst godlessness stirred a typical Jew to grief, wondering why God should show favour to such a "useless" nation. Some even complained, like the people during the prophetic era of Malachi (Malachi 3:13-18).

Jonah, just like a typical Jew, hated Nineveh so much, and the destruction of Nineveh would have been for him an event of great joy.

What were the sins of the Ninevites?

Though not specifically outlined it is not difficult to infer, just like the typical people of the time:

- Oppression of other nations.
- Sexual immorality and irresponsibility.
- Injustice and oppression of the poor, the needy, the defenceless.
- Paganic culture and idolatry.

God could no longer tolerate their wickedness and He sent Jonah to them. Imagine what happened? They believed God, and they repented. They didn't oppress Jonah, as many of us seek to harm those who challenge us. They didn't procrastinate; they didn't doubt the authenticity of the message. Their prosperity didn't blind them or harden their hearts. Their repentance seems more of a miracle.

The Bible says, *God saw what they did... He also repented of the evil with which He had threatened them.* Put differently, God was very impressed seeing their response (what a good thing to impress God. Can we think of anything in our lives that would impress God?).

Sin brings three things along with it, which are:

- Immediate Pleasure.
- Subsequent Sorrow.
- Eternal suffering.

The Lord called the Ninevites to change, to quit from sin at the moment of pleasure, before it graduates to sorrow and suffering. This they did without delay. They turned to the Lord in sorrow, even while in affluence, and the Lord turned to them in mercy, even when in anger.

In today's Gospel, Jesus began His preaching ministry. The heart of His message was "the kingdom of God is at hand, repent, believe in the Gospel."

As He proclaimed this message, He called His first four disciples. Every call demands that we leave something behind to answer it. Andrew and Simon left their nets; John and James left their father, the hired servants, the nets they were mending, their boat and followed Him.

Just as the Lord called these disciples, He is also calling us. To respond, we must leave something, we must abandon what we are doing at the moment, we must put an end to something.

Today, I will just mention four things the Lord is calling us to leave behind.

I.   *Every sinful association*

This means leaving behind membership of societies and associations that the Church forbids or discourages us from belonging to. The Lord is calling us to come out of the dark and walk in freedom with Christ, the light in the way of salvation. We must take this bold step today or else we will spend our lives in misery.

II.   *Every culture and tradition of paganism*

This means leaving behind every cultural practice that contradicts the Gospel truth; leaving behind every form of belief and practice, custom and tradition that betrays a hankering after idolatry or paganism. The Lord is calling us to boldly abandon them from today (Read Matthew 5:10-11).

III. Sinful relationships

The Lord is calling us out of every sinful relationship we might be in for whatever reason or excuse; every promiscuity, adulterous union, perpetual concubinage and fornication, illegitimate sexual union, friendship that corrupts, every relationship that contradicts purity and chastity, any bond that frustrates holiness and jeopardises our dignity as a child of God. The Lord is calling us out of it. We must be courageous like the Ninevites to tear the rope that has tied us in any unchristian bond.

IV. Unchristian lifestyle

There is a kind of lifestyle befitting of Christians. Christians are called to be like Christ.

What do we do that is inconsistent with the character of Christ? Let us ask ourselves today: How do I live? Where do I go? What do I do? What kind of person am I? Does my life reflect that I am a true child of God and a follower of Jesus? Where in my life have I failed to reflect Christ and witness to him?

The Lord is calling us today to come; please do not delay. The Second Reading tells us that the appointed time has grown very short; we should not harden our hearts, nor linger long in the wrong location and direction. Like the Ninevites, mercy is still calling; after mercy, judgement will call and with judgement comes punishment for all wrongdoings.

Again, I say to you, the Lord is calling us; delay no further.

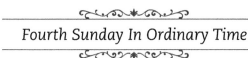
JESUS TAUGHT IN THE SYNAGOGUE

READING TEXTS:

DEUTERONOMY 18:15-20;
PSALM 95:1-2, 6-9; 1 CORINTHIANS 7:32-35;
MARK 1:21b-28

I am very happy to encounter the Gospel of today again on a Sunday. We read it some time ago, and today, I shall approach it gradually and then draw lessons simultaneously.

Jesus entered the synagogue and taught, and people were astonished because He taught with authority.

There was only one temple, which was in Jerusalem. The temple was the only centre of sacrifice and worship, whereas there were many synagogues. The synagogues existed principally for expounding the Torah. There was always a synagogue officer who appointed a scribe or a learned layman to explain the reading of the day.

Usually, the scribes explained the Torah by a secondary and derivative authority. What does this mean? They explained the Word of God by referring to the opinions of scholars in the school of Rabbis. Notable among those scholars were these three people; Gamaliel, Eleazar and Hillel. So, they used their ideas to explain the Word of God to the people.

In addition, the scribes would often explain the Word of God with care and fear; fear of other learned scribes, and care because often their lives did not match what they taught.

In the reading today, people went to the temple to hear the regular "according to Hillel", but beyond their expectation, they met Jesus in the temple. He did not teach about what others had said but in His own authority. Even the prophets always began with "thus says the Lord", but Jesus' preface was, *verily, verily, I say unto you..., you have heard how it was said, but I say to you...*

No one can explain a poem better than the author because whilst interpreters try to access and assess their intention, only they know what they have in mind. In the same way, Jesus Himself is the author of the Scriptures: they are the Word of God, He was God in human flesh.

Those who heard Him expound the Word of God were astonished; it was like they were hearing the voice of God on Sinai again. What an experience!

A man with an unclean spirit spoke out, and Jesus cast out the unclean spirit.

This was a very deep and profound event and there is a lot to learn here.

I.   *The Unclean Spirit*

When we talk of unclean spirits, many of us immediately

think of evil spirits and yes, that's true. An evil spirit can actually inhabit a body and torment the person and sometimes speaks through a person. Such spirits speak blasphemy about God, and about His ministers; they try to ridicule the power of God and the Church; they exaggerate their powers, try to threaten those around and accuse them. They operate by trying to destroy faith and courage and instill fear.

In dealing with them, we need to understand the fact that we are acting in the authority of Christ. We need patience and faith in the power of God at work through the sacramentals (crucifix, rosary, holy oil, holy water) and the powerful intercession of Mary.

However, there are other forms of unclean spirit present in many people in the Church. They are unclean spirits and we need to urgently apply Christ's help in exorcising them. Some of them include the spirit of anger, foul words, lying, stealing, pride, lust, unforgiveness/revenge, etc.

Let us cry to Jesus today, to use His authority to drive them out of us.

II. *The unclean spirit cried out*

Before now, the unclean spirit had been comfortable. Nothing had disturbed it, but today three things that can disturb an unclean spirit occurred.

- *The Spirit of God:* where the Spirit of God is present, unclean spirits cannot be comfortable. In Christ, we have the fullness of God's Spirit present. Anyone with God's Spirit becomes a terror to demons.
- *The Word of God:* where the Word of God is being preached in power and truth, it discomforts unclean spirits. It is a spirit of lies and deception. Unclean

11

      spirits are comfortable where there is insincerity, psyching, deception and fake ministration.

- *Holiness of life:* a holy person is a threat to unclean spirits. The holiness of Christ forced out the unclean spirit from his position of comfort.

When you combine these three things, you become a terror to unclean spirits: Spirit of God, knowledge of the Word of God, and holiness of life.

III. *What did the unclean spirit cry?*

"Ti hemin Kai soi " what have you to do with us...

Light and darkness can't exist together; put old wine in a new wineskin, and the wine will burst. This is a warning to those of us mixing our faith with "something else." What are light and darkness doing together?

Jesus of Nazareth? Have you come to destroy us? I know who you are, the Holy One of God.

The devil identified two things namely;

- The identity of Jesus.
- The superiority of Jesus.

IV. *The identity of Jesus*

The devil knew Jesus, even more than all those in the temple. He called Jesus by name, knew His hometown and His heavenly origin. The devil had a good knowledge of Christology, but it didn't change him from being a devil.

Many people have that kind of spirituality. We know all the answers to the catechism, we have memorised chunks of the Bible, we are acquainted with the Church's life, history,

Saints, theology but we are no better than demons.

Watch out, it is not what we know about God, but whether we know God, and knowing God can only be confirmed by our manner of living and the way we treat others.

V. *The superiority of Jesus*

The devil asked, *have you come to destroy us?* The devil acknowledged that Jesus was greater.

Often, we have Jesus, but we are still afraid. Today, the devil bowed to a greater power. Let us discover that in Jesus, we have a stronger side. David knew he had God on his side and his God was greater than the Goliath in front of him. While others were conquered by fear, David conquered fear with faith. Keep in mind that David was led by God's Spirit (1 Samuel 16:13) and reassured by God's Word (1 Samuel 17:45-47).

VI. *Jesus rebuked the unclean spirit: "silence and come out of him!"*

The Jews also had their practice of exorcism. It was usually a long process, somewhat like a magical rite to compel the spirit out of the possessed (Matthew 12:27). When Jesus rebuked the unclean spirit, he obeyed immediately. The words spoken were not ordinary (Psalm 33: 9). The same Word that created something out of nothing, the same Word that calmed the storm and raised the dead, was heard by the devil, and he gave the man a last "savage hug" and ran away.

The centurion confirmed this in Matthew 8:8: *...but only speak the Word, and my servant will be healed.*

13

May the Lord speak these words of healing, deliverance and transformation to our lives in Jesus' name. May the Word of God neutralise every negative word of men working against our lives. As we make use of the authority of God's Word, may every unclean spirit and power in our lives, begin to bow and be rendered powerless and harmless in Jesus' name.

*****

FOCUS ON GOD ALONE

READING TEXTS:
JOB 7:1-4, 6-7; PSALM 147:1-6;
1 CORINTHIANS 9:16-19, 22-13;
MARK 1:29-39

In the First Reading of today, we have Job reflecting on the mystery and misery of human life. Life is so full of challenges, disappointments, frustrations, fleeting joy and parading pains. This excludes no one, believers and non-believers alike.

Seeking lasting joy in this world is like trying to fish in a swimming pool. Let us keep in mind that the sorrows of this world should increase in us a longing for heaven, where we shall exchange the rugged cross of life, for a crown for all eternity.

In the Second Reading, St. Paul is teaching us something very important. He calls us to examine our attitude to our work, both spiritual and temporal. St. Paul tells us that preaching is a duty, a responsibility on him; a duty that he must fulfil and that he joyfully fulfils. He is not preaching for financial gain or self-seeking motives, but to please the

15

one who has sent him. As such, to fulfil his divine mandate, he chose to become all things to all men, that is, a slave of all.

At this point, we need to ask ourselves some salient questions:
How do I see my work (perception)? What drives me (motivation/intention)? How diligently and committed am I to tasks entrusted to me (disposition)?

Experience has taught us that many people, including believers, have a very poor, uncharitable, and irresponsible attitude to work. Some lack vision and are exclusively motivated by financial reward, and so have no sense of accountability and responsibility, and can't be trusted with significant tasks, assignments or responsibilities.

The life and words of St. Paul today call for sober reflection.

The Gospel of today is so rich. There is so much to talk about, but I just wish to discipline my thoughts and restrain myself to these three points:

1. Peter's mother-in-law began to wait on Jesus and the disciples after she has been cured. Her healing spurred her to service. She was cured of fever to use her strength to help others. Dear friends, you are blessed to bless others. We receive from God so that through us, others may be blessed too. Every privilege, opportunity and favour from God becomes a responsibility on us to become a channel for others to be lifted too.

2. Jesus cured many and cast out many devils. I want us to note that the Bible did not say all; it said many. This means that not all illnesses, problems and trials of life will disappear when we call on Jesus. Some sicknesses will remain despite all our novena,

16

because they have a place in the Master's plans for us. Some problems are meant to strengthen us, some to teach us lessons, some are necessary to purify us, some are just expiatory, that is, they are serving the cause of justice etc.

This leads us back to the First Reading. Whenever we pray, therefore, let us have faith and be hopeful, but most importantly, let us be open to whatever God in His goodness gives us. It is not every time that the Red Sea will part ways and it is not every wall of Jericho that will fall, because some are necessary to keep us in our place.

3. Everybody was looking for Him. Unlike us, Jesus always had time to be with God. He had no excuse of being busy or tired. After prayers, the disciples told Him that everyone was now looking for Him. That statement could have been a very strong temptation for Him to stay where He was loved and sought after.

   But like St. Paul in the Second Reading, Jesus wasn't motivated by fame, public attestation, comfort or money. All He cared about was doing His Father's will, as urgently and as best as He could.

Dear friends, let us not allow worldly praises, admiration, acceptance and commendation to distract our focus. Let us not become too comfortable and wish to remain in one place, when we are supposed to be on the move. Let us not remain in comfortable and open-handed Athens, when the Macedonians are also in dire need.

Let us be properly motivated in life by one thing: doing God's will; in the way He wills it to be done, as soon as He wants it done and wherever He wants it done.

JESUS CURED A LEPER

READING TEXTS:
LEVITICUS 13:1-2 ,44-46;
PSALM 32:1-2, 5, 11;
1 CORINTHIANS 10:31-11:1; MARK 1:40-45

Today is the Sixth Sunday in Ordinary Time, year B. The readings today are very instructive and inter-related. The Gospel narrates the cure of a leper and the details are very interesting.

Let me just bring out five points from the readings:

I.   *The faith of the leper*

Leprosy was believed to be inflicted on a person by God as a punishment for transgressions. Several cases abound in the Bible. Let me state three:

- King Azariah in 2 Kings 15:1-7
- Gehazi in 2 Kings 5:19-27
- Miriam in Numbers 12:1-15

It also means only God can cure someone of leprosy (check 2 Kings 5:6-7).

Today, this leper came to Jesus to ask for healing. He said, *if you will, you can make me clean.* He recognised the divinity latent in Christ's humanity. His leprosy didn't affect his faith. He believed that there was the power of God to do all things through Jesus. Do we also have faith in the power of God to help us in our present situation? Do we believe that if the Lord wills, He can help our present situation?

II. *His request depicts submission to God's will*

There is nothing God can't do (Psalm 115:3), but it is not everything He will do. There are times we ask for something and we don't get it. John the Baptist prayed inside the prison, but he never survived death by beheading. Is it that God can't do it? He did it for Peter, for Paul and Silas. In 2 Corinthians 12:7-10, St. Paul told us how he prayed three times for an intention, but he received the grace to endure rather than the removal of the affliction. Our prayers should recognise the fact that we request according to the limitation of our knowledge and reasoning, but God answers us according to His omnipotence and perfect wisdom and knowledge. In the long run, it should be: "Lord, if you will", and not "Lord, you have to."

III. *Jesus touched him*

The First Reading tells us how repulsive leprosy was. It excludes one from the community. Today, Jesus touched an outcast, He touched the untouchable. Is Jesus telling us something? He is telling us to stretch out our hands and touch those whom society rejects; those suffering from terrible sicknesses, those who have one defect or the other, those who have been stigmatised or whose images have been tarnished because of one atrocity or another that they committed. Let our feeling for them, be like that of Christ; not hatred, bitterness or repulsion, but compassion.

IV. *The man's disobedience*

Jesus gave this man an instruction; an instruction I won't call simple. He sternly charged him (*embrimeisamenos* - a strict warning) to say nothing to anyone. We are told that he went and talked about it freely (*keirussein*) and spread the news (*diapheimisein ton logon*). This means he wasn't just telling it to those who asked, he was proclaiming and announcing to whomever he met.

Two virtues we need to learn: prudence in words and obedience.

- We must learn how and when to keep quiet. It is not whenever we feel like talking that we should talk and it's not everything we feel like saying that we should say. We must be careful with the things we say when we are angry, excited, seeking favours, when we want to create an impression, when we want to court admiration or commendation from an authority figure or when we want to make people happy and laugh.
- We must learn to obey those that God has placed above us, especially in what doesn't offend our conscience. Obedience is a mark of humility, wisdom and discipline.

V. *Your good may bring troubles sometimes:*

In the long run, the kindness of Jesus to this man affected His ministry negatively. Jesus could no longer move freely. Mother Theresa once said that if you are doing good to people, many will misunderstand you and misrepresent your deeds, but then do good because, in the long run, it is about you and your God and not about you and them.

This is why the Second Reading tells us to do all we do to God's glory, because if we always expect gratitude from people, we may be disappointed and discouraged. Interestingly, this incident didn't stop Jesus from doing what was good. In fact, after this episode, almost immediately Jesus cured a paralytic at Capernaum (Mark 2:1 ff) and in chapter 3:1-12, He cured a man with a withered hand as well as many others.

Let us not allow the world to distract us from doing the good we know and that we have been called to do.

Happy Sunday to you all.

*****

SIN: THE GREATEST MADLADY

READING TEXTS:
ISAIAH 43:18-19, 21-22, 24b-25;
PSALM 41; 2 CORINTHIANS 1:18-22;
MARK 2:1-12

G race and peace from God the Father and the Lord Jesus be with you all. Dear friends in the Lord, today is the Seventh Sunday in Ordinary time, year B.

We are here today to give thanks to the Lord for His love and kindness, to worship the Lord and honour Him as our God, and in faith to present our needs to Him.

The readings of today are very comforting.

In the Gospel, we have an account of how Jesus forgave and cured a paralytic man, who was brought through the roof by his friends.

The faith and determination of the friends of the paralytic were very evident. They did everything possible to get him to Jesus; they were not discouraged by the obstacles they faced. They went as far as opening the roof of someone else's house.

However, when Jesus saw their faith, He said to the paralytic, *son, your sins are forgiven.*

His friends would have muttered, "please, he is paralysed, forget about his sins and heal him." Jesus knew his greatest need; sin is the greatest problem of humanity and mercy is our greatest need.

Of what good would it have been to have his two legs and walk right into hell. Forgiveness is the greatest miracle because it meets the greatest need.

The Pharisees who witnessed this were furious, and said, *only God can forgive sins, this is blasphemy.*

As a proof of His divinity, Jesus perceived in His spirit what they were pondering in their hearts, and to prove to them that He had the power to forgive sins, He told the man to stand up, pick up his mat and go.

They may not have been able to verify forgiveness and so He attested to it, by giving what they could verify. The power to heal and forgive belong only to God and so it meant that He was God.

Dear friends, the greatest problem we should be worried about is sin. Sin does more damage to us than any other thing.

Sin leads to a more calamitous paralysis; a spiritual paralysis. It incapacitates us spiritually, strains our relationship with God, hinders us from unrestrainedly blossoming spiritually. It threatens our salvation.

If only we knew the effect of one mortal sin, we would do everything possible to avoid it. St. Francis Xavier always said, "death rather than sin."

But here is the good news; in the First Reading, the Lord promises to do a new thing in our lives; He says the things of the past should not be considered again. The greatest blessing that God wants to give us is forgiveness and grace. He wants to deal with our greatest infirmity.

This is why He says: *I, I am He, who blots out your transgressions for my own sake, and I will not remember your sins.*

This mercy, restoration and grace are made possible in Christ Jesus. This is why St. Paul says in the Second Reading, *for all the promises of God find their Yes in Him.*

In this hope, let us approach the Lord today for mercy and forgiveness. When we are forgiven, we are healed from the root; we are made new and then we can become more alive, more fruitful, more productive in the Lord.

*****

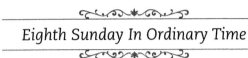

Eighth Sunday In Ordinary Time

THE QUESTION ON FASTING AND MATTERS ARISING

READING TEXTS:
HOSEA 2:16, 17cde, 21-22; PSALM 103;
2 CORINTHIANS 3:1b-6;
MARK 2:18-22

Dearly beloved in the Lord, grace and peace to you all. Today is the Eighth Sunday in Ordinary time, year B. In the Gospel account of St. Mark chapter 2, we have a record of four conflicts that the religious authorities had with Jesus.

Last week, we read the first one in Mark 2:1-12; they were angry that He forgave sin. Then in verses 13 to 17, they were upset that He associated with tax collectors and sinners.

Today, we have a report of the third conflict; He did not command His disciples to fast, and next week, we shall read the episode of the fourth conflict; He did not obey the sabbath (Mark 2:23-3:6).

So today let's focus on the third conflict with the Jewish authorities. They accused Jesus' disciples of not fasting as the Pharisees and the disciples of John did.

I need to quickly make this clarification. The law of Moses prescribed fasting only once a year, on the day of atonement (Leviticus 16:29, 23: 26; Numbers 29:7).

The Jews undertook a voluntary fast twice a week (Luke 18:12); on Monday and Thursday; the day Moses went to receive the law and the day he came back. So, it became a common pious act to fast twice a week.

Why did they fast?

Ordinarily, fasting is to express sorrow and humility before God, but the ritual fasting of the Jews was actually to prepare themselves for the coming Messiah; a Messiah who had come into their midst unknown to them.

Jesus responded to their accusations by using three analogies;

1. *The wedding guests cannot fast when the bridegroom is with them.*

    This implies that Jesus was the bridegroom and His disciples were the guests. His presence with them was a time of joy and celebration, while ritual fasting expressed sorrow and sobriety.

2. *No one sews a piece of unshrunk cloth on an old cloak.*

    If this is done, the patch pulls away from it, the new from the old, and a worse tear is made.

3.   *No one puts new wine into old wine skins.*

   If this is done, the wine will burst the skins
   and then the wine is lost.

In these analogies, Jesus intended to teach His questioners
that they cannot judge His new message with the old
traditional standard. He had come to fulfil the old and not
to be tied to it, and all those who wished to follow Him
could not cling to their old ways.

In the understanding of the Jews, the relationship with God
was principally based on works of the law; a strict
observance of the law and external practices. In the new
dispensation that Christ brought, emphasis is on grace; not
so much what we do for God but what God has done for us
in His Son.

This is why in today's First Reading, we see God promising
to transform, renew and restore His people. The emphasis
is on "I will"; what God will do and not what we shall do for
God. It is a righteousness based primarily on mercy and
grace, not on merit of works. Our work comes as a response
of love to an initiative of love taken by God.

Again, in the Second Reading, St. Paul reiterates this; we
cannot claim anything as coming to us based on merit; our
sufficiency and qualifications are gifts of grace.

There are so many lessons for us today. Let us ponder on
three:

I.   *We must not try to impose our spirituality on others.*

The Jewish authorities wanted Jesus' disciples to fast like
the Pharisees and the disciples of John. This is one
weakness of many pious brothers and sisters. They want

others to pray like them, practice their type of spirituality. If they pray silently, they are suspicious of those who pray loudly and if they pray loudly, they think others who pray silently are not spiritually connected. The fact that we say twenty decades a day, pray in tongues, and fast six days in a week, does not mean we should expect it of others. Grace is given to everyone in different proportion and God will not use our standards to judge others.

II. *Righteousness and justification are not fundamentally based on what we do for God.*

These are based on what God has done for us through Jesus Christ and what God is also willing to do for us. It is important for us to do some works, but they must be properly understood. We do not woo God by what we do; we do not "merit" salvation and God's pleasure simply by what we do. Our actions and spiritual exercises are just our response to God, who loves us beyond measure. Our hope is not in what we do for God but what He has done for us.

III. *The presence of Jesus is like the presence of a bridegroom; it is feasting all the way.*

Spirituality is not meant to make us sad, sober and sorrowful people, always gloomy and critical, seeing faults in everything and condemning everyone. True spirituality fills us with joy, and we radiate this joy to others. The presence of Christ in any soul brings about great joy and spiritual feasting. If our own relationship with God is mostly sombre and sepulchral, we need new wine and a new piece of cloth.

*****

RESPECT FOR THE DAY OF THE LORD

READING TEXTS:
DEUTERONOMY 5:12-15; PSALM 81;
2 CORINTHIANS 4:6-11;
MARK 2:23-3:6

G race and peace from God the Father and the Lord Jesus be with you all. Dear friends in the Lord, today is the Ninth Sunday in Ordinary time, year B.

In the Gospel of today, we have an account of the fourth conflict between Jesus and the Jewish religious authorities.

First, they accused Jesus' disciples of profaning the sabbath because they plucked heads of grain to eat. This, according to the custom, is doing work forbidden on the sabbath.

Secondly, they accused Jesus of curing a man with a withered hand on a sabbath.

Jesus responded to both allegations by taking them back to the original purpose of the sabbath which they had obfuscated by their customs.

In the First Reading we read about the essence of the sabbath. God Himself commanded that His chosen people should observe the sabbath as a day of celebrating His goodness, manifested in their deliverance from slavery. It was meant to be a day of rest, not just because the Lord rested on the seventh day from the work of creation, but fundamentally because the Lord wanted them to observe it as a day of rest, which was a sign of His goodness to them. In Egypt, they were unable to rest; they worked as slaves every day of the week, but now as people delivered and set free, they must rest.

The sabbath is a day of rest and because it is connected to what God did for them, it is a day to worship God.

Gradually, this meaning was lost as the Jews brought in excessive legalism which made the sabbath a day of slavery again. They lost the essence of the sabbath and burdened themselves by the rigorous and ultra-legal bonds tied to the sabbath.

Jesus has come to clarify lots of things; He wants us to understand what God really wants of us, how to please Him and to also minister God's mercy and kindness to us, which again is the spirit of the sabbath. He taught us two important lessons today:

I.   Any application of laws and customs at the detriment of human wellbeing is out of harmony with God's purpose.

II.   There is never a wrong day to do something good. No law should prohibit doing good for others.

As we learn from the Jewish misappropriation of the sabbath, we are also to reflect on our attitude to the day of the Lord. Sadly, many of us are no better than the Jews; though in a different dimension we have the same confusion.

They lost the essence of the sabbath in trying to preserve it; we also lose the essence of the sabbath in the way we treat it. Many people see the day of the Lord as merely a day to catch up with the things they are unable to do in the course of the week. For many others, there is no time for the Lord in the day of the Lord; it is a day to make extra money, to travel, have fun, go to a party, hang out with friends and nothing more.

Dear friends, our priority on Sunday should be to worship the Lord and be in communion with Him through prayers, meditation, and uniting with the faithful in sacred celebration. It is also a day to intentionally extend God's goodness to others and to rest from servile works.
It is called a day of the Lord.

*****

THE UNFORGIVABLE SIN

READING TEXTS:
GENESIS 3:9-15; PSALM 130:1-8;
2 CORINTHIANS 4:13-5:1;
MARK 3:20-35

Today, dearly beloved in Christ, I shall be preaching on what I title: *The Unforgivable Sin.*

Jesus tells us in today's Gospel that: *all of man's sins will be forgiven, and all their blasphemies; but let anyone blaspheme against the Holy Spirit and he will never have forgiveness: he is guilty of an eternal sin.*

The question is, "what is this unforgivable sin?"

Better still, why would sin be unforgivable? This concept of unforgivable sin seems to contradict the mystery of Divine Mercy and negate the grace of the Gospel dispensation.

For instance, God tells us in Isaiah 1:18, *Come now, let us set things right...though your sins are like scarlet, they may become white as snow; though they be crimson red, they may become white as wool.*

Here God promises to forgive all sins, of every shade and colour, big, small, original, actual, mortal, venial, red sins, white sins, crimson sins, scarlet sins.

Let's look at 1 John 1:9: *If we acknowledge our sins, He is faithful and just and will forgive our sins and cleanse us from every wrongdoing.*

So then, what is this unforgivable sin?

I once met a lady whom I noticed was always in a sober mood. She came to Church regularly but never received communion; she never came for confession and she wouldn't agree to perform any function in the Church.

On one occasion, after I had challenged her severally on her mood, she summoned up courage and told me after an evening mass that her attitude and mood were not willed, but as a result of the circumstances she found herself in. She told me that she had exceeded the elastic bounds of God's mercy. She had become pregnant and decided to have an abortion. Her sin had driven her to despair and caused her to give up hope of forgiveness.

What do you think? Could this be the unforgivable sin?

Could it be adultery or fornication which is a sin against our body, the temple of the Holy Spirit?

David committed this sin and then he was forgiven (2 Samuel 11). So, if you are here and you are thinking God cannot forgive you because you have been fornicating or committing adultery, you are wrong. If you repent, God will hastily forgive you.

Maybe this sin is even murder; to take the life of another person, in any form, even this is pardonable if we truly repent. A song goes thus, "a vilest offender who truly believes that moment from Jesus, a pardon receives..."

Look at Ahab for instance, after the cold murder of Naboth; he was still able to receive mercy (read 1 Kings 21:27-29).

So, is the unforgivable sin to speak rudely to God? To speak disrespectfully and faithlessly to God in distress?

Job did the same (Job 6:9-11, 10:18-22). The people of Israel did as much in the wilderness (Numbers 14:1-4) and during the prophetic age of Malachi (Malachi 3:14-15). Even these sins were pardoned.

So maybe idolatry? God detests idolatry so much. But then in Exodus 32, the people of Israel worshipped a golden calf and yet they received pardon when they repented (Exodus 32:14). No matter how we plunge ourselves into idolatry in all its different expressions, which includes visiting spiritualists, if we repent, the Lord is ready to forgive us, though we shall have to endure the just punishment due for our sins.

What of disobedience to God? Just as we have in today's First Reading, Adam and Eve disobeyed God. Yes, they were punished but they were also pardoned; their *necessary* sin gained for us so great a redeemer (exultet).

According to the teaching of the Church, the sins against the Holy Spirit which are neither pardonable in this world nor the next are the following:

I. *Presumption:*

This is to give ourselves false hope and misguided reliance

on the mercy of God; a vain thought that God is so merciful, He will find a way of saving me, He will not allow me to perish in my sin and so I have nothing to worry about, I can go on sinning. Check Sirach 5:5-7.

II. *Obstinacy in sin or final impenitence:*

This is when we continue to enjoy the delight of sin and refuse to repent despite all warnings. Final impenitence is to die without repenting of our sinfulness (Luke 13:3). This is a sin against the Holy Spirit because it is the Holy Spirit that convicts us of our sins and prompts us to repentance. This was the sin of the scribes from Jerusalem, who, despite all Christ did to call them to repentance, would not repent. Instead, they blasphemed and resorted to slander. There is no mercy, no forgiveness, no salvation without repentance.

III. *Despair:*

This is to lose hope of being saved and so disregard every means of mercy. This is also the sin of those who believe that they are not redeemable, they are not forgivable, and that they can never live righteously. Sometimes this drives people to suicide, believing their life is irredeemably worthless. This was the sin of Judas. To die in this state is to be forever doomed.

Dear friends, let us know that the mercy of God covers our past, present and future sins. The only one who cannot be pardoned is the one who has refused to repent or ask for mercy.

Happy Sunday to you all.

*****

THIS GOD

READING TEXTS:
EZEKIEL 17:22-24; PSALM 92:2-16;
2 CORINTHIANS 5:6-10;
MARK 4:26-34

Dearly beloved in the Lord, today is the Eleventh Sunday in Ordinary Time, year B.

The readings of today have a lot to tell us about God and our lives. After reflecting on today's reading, I just said unto myself, "this God, what an awesome God." This is why I titled my reflection: *This God.*

All the readings of today celebrate the awesomeness of God.

I will just enunciate three points about God for our meditation:

I. *It is the Lord who can promote, make us great, successful and announce us to the world.*

In the First Reading, the Lord says:

> *From the top of the cedar, from the highest branch, I will take a shoot and plant it myself on a very high mountain of Israel. It will sprout branches and bear fruit, and become a noble cedar...*

In a similar vein, the Gospel tells us that a farmer only plants; the seed grows not by his power, but the working of the one who has control of nature and has assigned laws of operation and existence to all He has created.

Many people in life, in the quest to be successful and great, recourse to all sorts of things, visit all sorts of places and associate with all kinds of beings, groups. Some people align themselves with secret societies, and illuminati. Many run faster and farther than their destiny.

We have stories of people who were once famous, recognised, celebrated but at the peak of their achievements, their secrets were exposed, and they came back to nothingness; from hero to zero.

As an example, let's read (at home) 2 Chronicles, chapter 22 to chapter 23. This tells us of Athaliah, who did everything to usurp the throne, including killing her children. She lasted for a while, but eventually she was shamefully deposed and killed.

Every greatness, increase and blessing sought outside of God will always and constantly end in regret.

The Bible also tells us of other people who are exalted by the Lord:

- *Gideon:* The Lord brought out Gideon from the weakest clan in Manasseh. He was the least in his family and God made him a conqueror (Judges 6:15).

- *David:* David, who was not even acknowledged by his immediate family, was made the greatest King in Israel (1 Samuel 16).
- *Mephibosheth/Meribaal:* 2 Samuel 9 tells us how God exalted a naked cripple, Mephibosheth and conferred on him a royal honour.

II. *It is the Lord who stunts tall trees (First Reading)*

A tall tree here depicts those who have power, who wield authority; those who are influential. Most specifically it is those who think as a result of their power and influence, they can do and undo. They can bring mountains low; they can repose, depose, oppress and go unchallenged.

An example here is the all-powerful Babylonian king named Nebuchadnezzar.

Nebuchadnezzar was arguably one of the most powerful kings that ever existed. He was a god-king and he conquered Assyria in their power; he destroyed Egypt in all might. Conquered nations Tyre, Judah, Damascus, and Sidon were all his vassal states. He was so powerful that he was represented as a lion with eagles wings (Daniel 7:4).

In Daniel 4:28-33, Nebuchadnezzar boasted, and God taught him a lesson. He reduced him totally to a beastly existence. This is an important lesson for all us of here today. If we think we can oppress people, we can make life miserable for them, if we think we have the power to decide who succeeds and who will fail, if we think we can thwart people's destiny, hinder people's progress in life, then we should learn from Nebuchadnezzar and be careful.

Another dimension to this is that when someone threatens to unjustly oppress, destroy or victimise us, we should run and cry to our God. There is no one that God created that God can't control or discipline.

III. *God is the one who judges*

The Second Reading completes our reflection on the omnipotence of God. It is to God that we shall all render an account of our lives. St. Paul tells us that each of us will be brought to the law court of God and we shall get what we deserve for the things we do, good or bad.

Connecting this with the Gospel, we can say that all our actions in life are comparable to someone sowing. The smallest seed we sow will germinate and become a big tree.

Those who have resolved to spend their lives doing good are sowing and in due time, they will reap. Those who have resolved to spend their lives doing evil, will also reap.

Keep three things in mind:

- Every action we do, we are sowing, and we shall only reap what we sow.
- There is no one that God can't call to question and order.
- God will indeed judge everyone and repay all our actions in the body.

Happy Sunday to you all.

*****

Twelfth Sunday In Ordinary Time

PEACE, BE STILL

READING TEXTS:
JOB 38:1, 8-11; PSALM 107;
2 CORINTHIANS 5:14-17;
MARK 4:35-41

Dear friends in the Lord, may the peace and love of the Lord Jesus, which surpasses all human understanding fill your hearts. Today is the Twelfth Sunday in Ordinary time, year B.

We have a very powerful Gospel today, so rich and deep.

St. Mark narrates an episode which has so much to teach us; an incident which shows the humanity and divinity of Jesus, His care for us, and His power over nature.

Jesus told the disciples, *let us go across to the other side.* On the way, they faced the threat of an awful storm. All the while, Jesus was asleep on the cushion; it must have been a deep sleep for Him not to notice the great gale and the waves.

The disciples were completely terrified, and they woke Him up and said: *Teacher, do you not care that we are perishing.*

Jesus woke up and rebuked the wind, and said to the sea, *Peace! Be still!*

At His command, immediately, the winds became calm, the waves settled, the storm passed.

He then turned to His disciples and asked, *why are you afraid? Have you still no faith?* That is, do you not know who I am? Do you think I will be in this boat and you will perish? Do you really think I do not care about you?

This is what Jesus is saying to someone today. Why are you afraid? Why do you think I do not care? Why do you question my love for you? Why do you think I am not with you? Why are you afraid that things will go wrong even when I am with you? Do you not know the God you serve?

After everything, the disciples were filled with awe and they said to one another, *who then is this, that even the wind and the sea obey Him?*

They knew that no mere mortal could silence the wind and the sea, that no human being, no matter how holy, could control nature. Only God our Creator, can command natural forces and restore order in that manner. This is why they marvelled, *what manner of man is He?*

Thank God, we know the answer:

He is a Man-God or better still a God-Man, in whose hands are the depths of the earth, the heights of the mountains are His, to Him belongs the sea for He made it and the dry land shaped by His hands (Psalm 95:3-5).

In today's First Reading, the Lord revealed His greatness to Job. He revealed Himself as the one who shut in the sea with doors, who made garments for the clouds, who prescribed bounds for the sea. He is Lord God the Almighty.

What is the Lord teaching us today?

I.   He is always present in whatever we go through (Isaiah 43:2). We are never alone.

II. When He is with us, we have nothing to be afraid of. He will not watch us perish. Jesus cannot be in a boat and the passengers perish. Jesus cannot inhabit a place and its indwellers be doomed. His presence makes a difference.

III. We should never think He does not care because He does (1 Peter 5:7). His care does not mean we won't go through storms; it means He will help us through it.

IV. Our God has power and control over all situations. We are serving a mighty God. A situation may be out of our control, we may be helpless, but no situation is out of His control, and He is never helpless.

V.   If the sea and winds obey His voice, why should we not? If nature responds to His command, why should we not?

*****

JAIRUS AND THE WOMAN WITH THE HAEMORRHAGE: AN ENCOUNTER THAT MAKES A DIFFERENCE

READING TEXTS:
WISDOM 1:13-15; 2:23-24;
PSALM 30:2, 4-12;
2 CORINTHIANS 8:7, 9, 13-15; MARK 5:21-43

Dearly beloved in the Lord, today is the Thirteenth Sunday in Ordinary Time, year B.

In today's Gospel, we are being presented with two dramatic miraculous deeds: the raising to life of Jairus' daughter and the cure of the woman suffering from haemorrhage.

Let's begin by looking at the characters of today:

I. *Jairus:*

He was a synagogue official, and of course, a wealthy man. He belonged to the class of people who were not always on good terms with Jesus. His circumstances led him to Jesus. He came as a man desperately in need. His daughter was sick, and they had tried all the physicians and medicines but there was no improvement, and now his daughter was at the point of death. He must have heard about Jesus and in desperation applied himself to Him. His experience reminds us that God often uses our cross to draw us to Himself.

II. Jairus' daughter:

She was just twelve years old, the darling of the house; pretty, intelligent, very promising, a lovely angel, the favourite of her father, with the promise of womanhood ahead of her. Now, sickness had gripped her and was dragging her hastily to the abode of death. All her ambitions died with her and the hope that she would one day bring her family glory also died with her.

(Prayer: May we not die before our time; may death not pluck our flowers when they are about to blossom).

III. The Haemorrhaging Woman:

She had had a flow of blood for twelve years. A normal flow should be three to seven days, meaning she had suffered this for 4,380 days. Let us examine what she had suffered. She had been to several physicians. Imagine the shame of repeating herself to several physicians and being "thoroughly" examined again and again. If this was in Africa, friends would have advised her to visit spiritualists and say that it was not a hospital issue.

I suppose she must have visited different grades and classes of spiritualists, offered all sorts of sacrifices, bathed in assorted rivers, and swallowed tons of concoctions. Of course, she would have paid the spiritualist for all these, but it had all been to no avail.

Now, this woman had nothing left to spend and she had given up. She had given up hope. She had sold her assets and exhausted the money on her sickness, but the sickness didn't end. Her husband remarried because only a few men understand the concept of "for better for worse"; many men can endure other things but not abstinence.

She suffered terrible stomach pains. This sickness had embittered her comfort, and she had lost so much blood that gradually she was being dragged to her death, hopeless and helpless.

Spiritually, it was a worse situation, as she could not participate in public worship and could not relate properly with people, because she remained "ritually unclean", she and anyone who touched her.
(Cf Leviticus 15:25-27).

In the midst of this, I am very impressed with this woman, you know why? She didn't commit suicide. In our days, suicide seems to have a strong attraction.

Please help me preach a little: tell your neighbour, "suicide is not an option." Jesus says, *there is hope for you.*

While people could approach Jesus publicly stating their needs, this woman couldn't say hers openly, it was something so shameful. Do you know that kind of sickness? Perhaps something like that is wrong with some of us right here and now; things we can't say out loud.

Similarities in the Healing

- Both cases were hopeless. This woman had tried everything humanly possible. Jairus had consulted the best physicians. In fact, in the case of Jairus, his daughter even died before Jesus got there and we are told "if there is life, there is hope" and that "it is sickness one cures and not death."

- They were both unworthy of help: Why? Jairus belonged to a class of people that Jesus should have treated as enemies. He also came on behalf of a girl. Girls/women didn't have such importance in the patriarchal Jewish society. More so, being dead, Jesus ought not to have touched her lest He became unclean for seven days. The person suffering from haemorrhage was first a woman and secondly unclean. She should not have even been in such an assembly at all, under pain of death. No wonder, she was afraid of what she had done.
- They came to Jesus with faith. Jairus believed in Him. The woman, after touching many things in life and after being touched by many things/people, still believed if she could just touch His garment, she would be well.

Let us look at the hero of the day, the final and greatest character. Let someone shout "Jesus."

IV. *Jesus:*

Jesus is a specialist in difficult and hopeless cases. When other helpers fail and comfort flees, He is the help of the helpless. Can you imagine the joy of the woman? In an instant, the disgraceful malady left her after twelve years.

Can you imagine the joy of Jairus and his household? His daughter was called back from the grip of death, from the captivity of the grave. She didn't just rise but rose and walked, to show she was restored not just to life, but to good health as well.

Today's Psalm is their Psalm.

The daughter of Jairus sang the first stanza of today's Psalm. It was just the Psalm for her. Jairus sang the second stanza. The woman "FORMERLY" suffering from haemorrhage, sang the last stanza and with tears, she ended:

for me you have changed my mourning into dancing. O Lord my God, I will thank you forever.

The First Reading tells us that suffering, disease, and death come to us, not because of God's wickedness, but because of the fall/disobedience of the first Adam. However, this has been conquered by the second Adam, who came to take our infirmities away, bear our diseases and give us life. He helps all in need, not minding whether they are worthy or not.

In the Second Reading, we see the Spirit of Christ in the Corinthians, that spirit of charity that extends to the undeserving. The Corinthians, who were essentially Romans and Greeks, were helping their brethren in Judea, even at a time when antisemitism and racio-cultural disparity was common-placed. Helping the underserved is the Spirit of Christ.

Message For Today

1. What is our haemorrhage today? What is bringing us shame? What is it that if Jesus were to take it away, would make us most happy? If Jesus were to be here, what would we ask?

   Here is the good news, Jesus is here now, so ask. You have the opportunity of not just touching His garment but receiving Him; ask with faith here and now (see John 11:40).

Our Faith will make the difference. I say to us all today: "there is hope of glory, a miracle of grace, and blessings that beat imagination awaiting us, only in Christ Jesus."

2. Jesus helped those who were most undeserving of help. He didn't allow racial prejudice, ideological differences, or cultural bias to be obstacles.

Like Jesus today, let us not refrain from helping those in need just because of our differences. As Jesus told us all in the parable of the good Samaritan, anyone who is in need is our neighbour, and we must help him/her (Luke 10:25-37).

Happy Sunday to you all.

*****

THE PLACE OF THE CROSS

READING TEXTS:
EZEKIEL 2:2-5; PSALM 123:1-4;
2 CORINTHIANS 12:7-10;
MARK 6:1-6

Today is the Fourteenth Sunday in Ordinary Time, year B. It's another opportunity for us to thank God, to hear the Word of God and to receive abundant blessings.

However, I wish to begin my reflection from the Second Reading, which is a complete spiritual meal, and a balanced diet at that. (However, I shall share my thoughts on the First Reading and Gospel and seek to connect them).

St. Paul gave us lots to ponder on from his experience. God used St. Paul to work so many miracles. His prayers were efficacious and through him, many experienced God's grace upon their lives.

Let me just share some cases from the Bible:

- At Lystra, God used him to make a crippled man walk (Acts 14:8 ff).
- God cast out a spirit of divination through him (Acts 16:16-18).
- God raised Eutychus to life through him (Acts 20:7-12).
- In Acts 19:11-12, we learnt that even his face towel and aprons worked miracles.

Having established these facts about Paul, we find him today, in a situation that he doesn't love but he is powerless to change.

I. *Everyone has a cross*

Even Paul had his cross. The person helping others to carry theirs, had his own cross. Even Simon of Cyrene, who helped Jesus to carry His cross, had his cross. Even if we don't know anything else about him, we know Simon was from Cyrene, modern-day Libya, on the Northern coast of the African Continent, which was under Roman governance. He belonged to a race and a people treated by the Romans as sub-humans. To come from a despised race or family, isn't that enough of a cross?

So, we ought not to think we are the only one carrying a cross. Some people's crosses are manifest, some people's crosses are latent. The fact that one is manifest doesn't mean it is heavier than those who bear secret crosses.

There is never a time when we won't bear a cross in life; we will only be relieved of one, to then carry another. There is never a state of cross-lessness; that is the state that many Christians desire and this is why we spend our lives in sorrow, chasing what we cannot achieve.

II. Not all burdens will be removed.

There are certain things and realities in our lives that we are not comfortable with; they make us weep, and we wish we could change them. We have even tried to change them ourselves, either through our efforts or through prayers, but they have remained unmoved.

Sometimes, it could be sickness, weakness or a bodily defect. It could be a family problem, a deformity in our physiological configuration, a blessing not received. Sometimes what we receive is not what we bargained for. We can describe these realities as thorns in our flesh.

For St. Paul, it was not stated but there are many conjectures. Some said it was sickness, some that it was something that impeded his speech, and some said it was the pain of the disappointments he received from the Church he established.

Whatever it was, it must have been something humbling and grievous, something that frustrated and caused discomfort and displeasure in his life.

In addition to this, we are told that an Angel of Satan beat him up. He prayed to God three times (three times here means severally), but still this didn't stop.

Dear friends, not every problem in our life will be removed. We will have to manage some. We will have to accept some.

Prayers are efficient, necessary and powerful but they are not meant to control God; they are to acknowledge our needs and express our dependence on God.

God answers all prayers of faith, but He answers according to His loving plans. We often pray from the limitation of our knowledge and experience, but the God, who will grant our prayers, is all-knowing, all-powerful and all good.

To balance our prayers, we must not just command God to give us what we desire, we must desire what He gives us too. St. Paul asked for a removal of thorns, and God gave him the graces to bear his burden. Why didn't God just remove this thorn and command an end to Paul's plight? This leads us to my third point.

III. *Often our crosses have their place in our Christian journey.*

St. Paul recognised the spiritual significance of this cross and this gave him peace and comfort. It was meant to stop him from being proud.

Someone I know gave birth to a child with Downs Syndrome, after some years of waiting on the Lord. She prayed so much for God's healing for her son, but things grew worse. She became angry with God, but eventually, she resolved to care for the child to the best of her abilities. In doing so, she developed a great love for the child. Later, she resigned from her job to care for the child and she felt so fulfilled doing this. She accepted it joyfully from God and in time, she realised her vocation - her calling was to help children with such defects.

This is God at work. This has drawn her closer to God and made her a source of blessings to many others, something she wouldn't have imagined previously.

Simon of Cyrene was compelled before he carried Jesus' cross, but eventually, it was to his benefit. He didn't like the cross, but it was a privilege that God gave him. He touched Jesus' broken body and thick-flowing blood; he participated in the redemption of humanity, and he also shared in the fruit. According to extra-biblical sources, he became a believer after the resurrection, and converted his whole family (some refer to Romans 16:13 to buttress this).

IV. Glory in the cross

There is glory in the cross, although it takes grace and faith to identify this. When we realise this, we find inner peace. St. Paul found peace when he discovered the glory in his cross. He says:

I shall be very happy to make my weaknesses my special boast, so that the power of Christ may stay over me, and that is why I am quite content with my weaknesses, and with insults, hardships, persecutions…

Note the progression in Paul's disposition, from complaint and prayers for the removal of thorns, to joyous acceptance and gratitude.

Dear friends, two things we must pray for from today:

- The vision of faith to see God in our crosses.
- The grace to accept and bear our crosses with peace, patience and gratitude.

Meditation on the First Reading and the Gospel

The First Reading of today tells us about God's mandate to Ezekiel. Let's examine the context. God's spirit made him stand up and God told him: *I am sending you to the Israelites, to the rebels who have turned against me.*

God sent him to rebels, who were defiant and obstinate. He told Ezekiel whether they listened or not, he should warn them. This call happened just four years after their Babylonian captivity. Ezekiel was among the exiles. His ministry was between 593-571. He was to tell them that their sins were the cause of their exile and that worse things would happen if they did not repent; that Jerusalem and the temple would be destroyed.

Does anyone think this was going to be an easy mission for Ezekiel? He suffered so much in carrying out this mission; he was despised, hated, rejected and punished because of his message. The difficulties associated with his ministry were his own cross, which he had to carry faithfully to receive a reward for obedience from God.

Like Ezekiel, Jesus was rejected by His own people. Just as the Gospel account of St. John foretold, He came to His own and His own received Him not (1:11). This was a cross in the life of Jesus. He preached in the synagogue of His own country and He was despised, treated with contempt and they took offence at Him. He marvelled at their lack of faith. The Greek word is *ethaumazen,* which connotes the idea of being embarrassed, offended, at a loss for words.

No matter our cross in life, let us not forget what is most important; God knows what is best for us and His grace is sufficient for us. Like Samuel we could learn to always say: *He is the Lord; let Him do what seems good to Him* (1 Samuel 3:18).

*****

SHARING IN THE MISSION OF CHRIST JESUS

READING TEXTS:
AMOS 7:12-15; PSALM 85:9-14;
EPHESIANS 1:3-14;
MARK 6:7-13

Dear friends in Christ, today is the Fifteenth Sunday in Ordinary time, year B. We thank God for His goodness in our lives. As we prepare to hear the Word of God, let us confess that the Word of God has the power to transform, and ask that it be done to us according to our faith.

My reflection today is titled: *Sharing in the mission of Christ Jesus.*

Gladness filled my heart as I read today's reading and I feel it speaks to me more than anyone else. To be able to pay attention to its significant detail, I would like to approach it by way of exegesis.

Mark 3:13-15 tells us that Jesus called His disciples to be with Him, so that He might send them out and give them authority over unclean spirits. They had now been with Him for approximately six months. They had sat at His feet, learnt His doctrines, seen His miracles and now He was sending them out as "teaching practice."

I will just draw our attention to five details from the text and these shall be our message for today.

I. He sent them out in pairs.

Jesus sent these men out in pairs. They had to learn to work together. Although they were different in orientation, background and temperament, they were united in a singular mission. They needed each other's talents, gifts and companionship. They needed to pray together, encourage, support and strengthen one another.

Today, it's so difficult for two people to live or work together; president and vice-president of a pious group at loggerheads; the chairman of the council at war with his Parish Priest; the difficulties of two ministers of God living together; husband and wife supposed to be companions, conspicuously divided in heart, mind and will; one group against another in the same Church. Yet we claim to belong to the same Christ and share the same vision and mission.

Dear friends, we must learn to support each other, and tolerate each other. We must learn that we need each other, and we must learn to reconcile all our differences. Christ should be the centre of our unity and our common affiliation to Him should dissolve all our differences.

II. He gave them authority

It's so interesting to note that the men Jesus sent out were incompetent. They were still struggling to understand Him, His teaching and lifestyle. They were still very inadequate. If you just read Mark 8-9 alone, you will see how they were still struggling to catch up with their lessons. Here are some examples:

- In Mark 8:4, they were confused on how to feed a crowd of four thousand; they still didn't understand that God can do anything.
- In Mark 8:14-18, He chastised them for ignorance and wrong interpretation of simple admonition.
- In Mark 8:31-33, they didn't grasp the mystery of His redemptive suffering and Peter, their spokesman, got a hot rebuke.
- In Mark 9:10, they didn't even understand the basic salvation truth of the resurrection.
- In Mark 9:14-29, they were embarrassed for not being able to cure a boy with a spirit.
- In Mark 9:33-37, they had a gossip which betrayed their love of power and dominance.
- In Mark 9:38-39, they wanted to stop someone who was doing good but had not registered with their union.

Take note, all these took place within a short space of time (2 chapters). This shows us that they were still far from adequate, but then Jesus gave them authority and they did well. He commissioned them to attack the devil's kingdom, to cast him out of the body of those who were possessed, and they succeeded.

Sometimes we feel overwhelmed by our weaknesses and inadequacies and we are quick to reject the work /assignment of God, because we are convinced that we are incompetent. No one is competent or qualified for God's work of any sort (cf 2 Corinthians 3:5), however, our incompetence should never be an excuse if God is the one sending us. He gives us authority and grace (Romans 8:30).

In today's First Reading, Amos told Amaziah that he was just a shepherd who was sent by God to go and prophesise.

This implies that his authority and qualification came from God.

Isaiah, in the reading of yesterday, is another case study (Isaiah 6:1-8). When God calls us for any task, we must learn to accept in humility and gratitude. When we feel overwhelmed by its enormity and the limit of our capacity, we must learn to rely on the authority and grace of the one who has called us.

III. *He gave them instructions*

Jesus gave them instruction on how to carry out this mandate. They were to go with only walking sticks and sandals, no extra clothes, no purse, no food or money. They were not to look for a comfortable apartment by sampling houses.

Why these kinds of instructions?

- Jesus wanted them to appear like the common men that they were being sent to. They were to appear as simple as the village folks they would minister to and were to learn poverty of spirit.
- Jesus wanted them to know that the ministry was not about comfort. If there was any comfort, it was the comfort of gaining souls for Christ.
- Jesus wanted them to rely on God for their needs. They needed to learn to trust God and believe that He would take care of them.

This has so much to say to us (as ministers) on the need to learn to be simple, to shun materialism and to imbibe poverty of spirit.

However, since I am not preaching to priests, as people of God too, the Lord is teaching us not to look down on others, not to act and dispose of ourselves as if we are better than them. Often, we inflate our personality and we want to impress on others that we are better, whether in worldly standards or piety. We should, therefore, shun all self-righteousness and aura of superiority. This is antithetical to an evangelical spirit. We must always acknowledge that we are products of grace and we are nothing without grace.

We must also learn to depend on God to take care of our needs. We must learn to worry less and have confidence that our God cares for us and He is more than able to supply our needs (Philippians 4:19).

Being a Christian also brings its hardship. Sometimes we have to bear some painful circumstances; we have to endure hardships, denial, rejection and discomfort. It is a call to carry a cross, that leads to life.

Faith and commitment consist in being able to endure hardships and difficulties with patience, submission and gratitude in union with Christ Jesus.

St. Paul told the elders of Ephesus that he was aware that persecutions and imprisonments were ahead of him, but then what was important was to carry out the mandate he had received from Christ (Acts 20:22-24).

IV. *Response to rejection.*

Jesus was aware that although the disciples would come as simply as possible with a message of hope and salvation, they would still be rejected.

He taught them what to do. They should do as the Jews did. Whenever the Jews returned from a journey to a pagan land, before they crossed back into Israel, they would shake the dust off their clothes and their shoes. It represented a total dissociation from the pagans and the pollution of their lands.

Jesus told them to use this sign against those who rejected the message of salvation. They were the true pagans and since they had rejected God's offer of salvation, by that very fact, they had accepted the sentence of damnation. They rejected God's message to their peril.

This was the case with Amaziah in the First Reading, who rejected God's call to repentance through Amos, and instead he resorted to hostility, antagonism and conspiracy.

Are we like the pagans who reject God's message? Every Word of God we hear is both a privilege and a responsibility. We also have the freedom to accept or reject it. However, for whichever choice we make, there is a consequence.

Hardheartedness, fearlessness, presumption and obstinacy in sin will drive many to share in the lot of Sodom and Gomorrah. The reality and truth of salvation and damnation, heaven and hell will dawn suddenly on so many, and it will be too late to repent and to give excuses for wasted opportunities of repentance.

V. *The performance of the disciples*

We are told the disciples set off to preach repentance: and they cast out many devils and anointed many sick people with oil and cured them. The ministry of Jesus was their ministry. They were to duplicate Jesus' ministry and Jesus was very happy that they were doing it; that they were expanding the kingdom of God.

Two points I want to draw from here:

- Jesus' attitude challenges us to shun all forms of envy and feelings of insecurity and threat from the success of others. Many people do not want those under them to be as good as they are, never mind be better.

  That is not the spirit of Jesus; it is the 'Saulic' spirit; Saul, who saw David's success as a threat to his fame. Jesus even tells us in John 14:12, that to those who believe in Him, He will give the power to do greater works.

  This is a sign of spiritual and affective maturity; to rejoice seeing that people under you, younger than you or trained by you, are doing well or even better.

- The mission of Jesus is our mission too. As Christians, we are called to share in the mission of Christ. The essence of the mission is not to perform miracles but to witness to others through words, works of love and the sympathetic influence of a good life.

That is what the Second Reading tells us. We have been blessed with all spiritual blessings. We have been called and chosen in Christ. We are chosen to know the mystery of salvation, and to accept the message of truth. We are stamped with the seal of the Holy Spirit, all for His kind purpose.

What is that purpose? To share in the mission of Christ; that is, the business of saving souls.

To save a soul is one of the greatest miracles God can perform through us.

Happy Sunday to you all.

THE MAKING OF A RESPONSIBLE SHEPHERD

READING TEXTS:
JEREMIAH 23:1-6; PSALM 23:1-6;
EPHESIANS 2:13-18;
MARK 6:30-34

There is so much poverty in our world today. The poverty is of different sorts. There is economic poverty which we are all familiar with and are directly or indirectly suffering from, however there are more dangerous kinds of poverty ravaging human life.

Let me just highlight 4 more kinds of poverty here:

- Poverty of commitment.
- Spiritual poverty.
- Poverty of love.
- The poverty of responsibility.

This morning I shall be preaching on this last point; the poverty of responsibility or you may say the poverty of responsible men and women. The population of the world is increasing daily and yet responsible people are reducing day by day. We have an overflow of irresponsibility in every sector of human life.

We have tons of irresponsible leaders, irresponsible politicians, irresponsible bosses and managers, so many irresponsible lecturers and heads of institutions, departments and faculties. We have irresponsible people in different vocations, careers and professions.

We have husbands who are irresponsible towards their fundamental responsibilities. We have wives and mothers who have awards in maternal irresponsibility. We also have irresponsible children who despite the toils of their parents, have chosen a path of stupidity, gambling, waywardness and gross irresponsibility.

The most painful of all is that we also have irresponsible religious leaders and ministers. Spiritual leaders who have lost sense of their mission, are lacking in integrity and moral probity, who have lost track of their vision and ideals, and who pervert the Gospel; leaders who project the self above the flock, shepherds who care for themselves at the detriment of their sheep, leaders lacking in knowledge, spirituality, character and definitive human virtues.

The readings of today call us to reflect on whether we are responsible, or we are irresponsible people and leaders.

God says, *doom for the shepherds who allow the flock of my pasture to be destroyed and scattered.*

These are shepherds who instead of taking care of the sheep, feed on them and do not care for them, thereby allowing them to wander.

God says: *right now, I will take care of you for your misdeeds.* To take care here means "I will deal with you."

The Gospel presents Jesus to us as the shepherd who cares first for His disciples and then the people, and He was ready to sacrifice His comfort and rest to take care of their needs out of genuine sympathy.

The questions we shall ask ourselves today are:

Am I a responsible man/husband at home? Am I a responsible wife, woman and mother at home? Am I a responsible leader of my association, group or organisation? Am I a responsible boss, manager, lecturer, teacher, nurse, doctor? Am I a responsible worker or staff member? Are we responsible parents? Am I a responsible Elder? Am I a responsible in-law? Am I a responsible priest?

From all the readings of today let's identify five key indications of a responsible person:

I.   A responsible person/leader cares for and is sensitive to the needs of those under his/her watch. He knows what they need and makes an effort to meet it.

     Jesus knew the disciples would be tired. He knew the people needed a shepherd. He knew what they needed, and He didn't wait to be told. Though they came for more miracles, He decided to teach them because that's what they needed.

     In doing that, He fulfilled the Psalm of today; He spread the spiritual banquet table, He led the lost sheep into the green pastures of His soothing words, He caused them to lie down beside the still waters of His wonderful blessing.

     We are told that Jesus was moved with compassion; *esplanchnisthe*, that is a sympathetic feeling that starts in the deepest region of a person's being; a sincere feeling of pity and a willingness to help.

Many of us today are guilty of apathy, that is the absence of emotion. We see the needs, but we do not care. We do not care for those around and under us.

There is so much hunger, tears, sorrow and depression around, but we fail to notice, we notice and are unmoved and sometimes we justify our indifference.

II. A good shepherd is one who is approachable, available and accessible. Take note that Jesus and His disciples wanted to be alone by themselves to eat and rest. However, when confronted by human needs, about 15,000 to 20,000 people who had walked about ten miles, Jesus set Himself to teach them.

How many of our religious leaders, political leaders and even bringing it closer to home, how many of us are available to our families and children and are accessible and approachable to those around us? We may often be high up there, frowning, aggressive, light tempered and scary. Are you approachable, accessible and available to those whom God has placed under your watch?

III. A responsible shepherd/leader/person sets a good example. Many of us teach by precepts, not by example. Jesus didn't just teach us to love, to be humble or care for others; He showed us. How many of us are living exemplary lives? How many of us can we call sources of inspiration? Spiritual models? How many of us are treading the path of virtue and integrity, leaving heroic legacies behind? How many of you want your children to become like you? What example are we giving the world? What will the world look like if everybody becomes like us?

IV. A responsible shepherd is one who sacrifices for the welfare of those under his care. Many of us today are so self-centred. We seek our own interest even at the detriment of others. We are ready to make others sacrifice to meet our needs, but we find it difficult to sacrifice and bear any inconvenience for the sake of others.

We see Jesus today, tired and hungry; He could have responded with anger to the unexpected demands on His ebbing energy. He sacrificed His comfort for them. This is what the bad shepherd in today's First Reading won't do.

According to today's Second Reading also, He made the supreme sacrifice which restored peace among divided people. He offered His own body as a sacrifice to break down the barrier erected between the Jews and gentiles.

How willing are we to sacrifice for others to have comfort, joy and to live again?

If you were asked to donate blood or one of your vital organs to restore someone to health, you might well find every reason to say "NO!" Whereas if you are the one in need, you would hope that everyone would donate theirs. Whenever we find it difficult to suffer or lose something for someone, let's take a look at the crucifix and see someone who donated not just an organ but the whole of Himself for us. How sacrificial are we for others?

V. A responsible person is one who sets time aside to be alone with God, to examine himself, to re-evaluate his life and commitments with the consciousness that one day he will render a full and detailed account to God, just as the apostles rendered account to Jesus today.

In conclusion, the readings of today are not just a challenge to us but there is also the dimension of consolation. Jesus is the good shepherd who knows our needs and cares for us; Jesus cared for the people, not just as a crowd, but individually. He knows the needs of all. He saw the individuals in the crowd. As you are here listening to me, God sees not just a congregation but all of us as individuals.

He sees every broken heart, every physical ailment, every emotional need, every spiritual problem. He sees our sick children, He sees the abused wife, He sees the depressed father. He sees our disappointment, frustrations and how doubt threatens to destroy our faith. He sees our painful struggles; He sees how we struggle to deal with our imperfections even though everyone is condemning us. He sees what we are going through on account of our children, He sees how sad we are and the trace of our tears even though we try to use makeup to cover it up. He sees the agony we go through in the garden of our home, He sees the scourging at the pillar by our in-laws, He sees the crown of thorns placed on our head by those we trusted. He sees the heaviness of the spiritual, financial, psychological and emotional cross we carry. He sees how people have crucified us despite our innocence.

Jesus says to you today, "don't breakdown, I care for you; no matter your imperfections and moral weaknesses, I will never ignore you in your misery."

Take a deep breath and say after me:

Thank you, Jesus, for your care for me. Teach me to understand that I am not alone, that you are with me. Help me to be responsible and to extend your love and care to others in their moments of need. Amen.

*****

Seventeenth Sunday In Ordinary Time

JESUS FED THE MULTITUDE

READING TEXTS:
2 KINGS 4:42-44; PSALM 145:10-18;
EPHESIANS 4 1-6;
JOHN 6:1-15

Sometimes, we find ourselves in a situation where we can't see any solution or hope, even though we may be praying. We can't see any possibility that things can turn out in our favour again.

Then suddenly, the unexpected begins to happen, eventualities beyond our imagination, and in our bewilderment, we are like "Wow! God, you are great!"

This is the kind of situation that we have in the Gospel and the First Reading.

Last Sunday, we took our Gospel reading from the Gospel account of St Mark 6:7-13. Jesus wanted to rest; a crowd followed Him, and He set Himself to teach them.

Today, we continue the incident that Mark narrated, but now from the account of John. We read the Gospel from

68

John 6:1-15. For the next five Sundays, we shall be reflecting on these Johannine series.

Today, we have the story of the feeding of five thousand men. To be more realistic, we should say the feeding of about 20,000 people with five barley loaves and two fish. Let us examine the events more closely.

Jesus continued to teach the people for so long. The disciples were getting worried and discussing among themselves, "when will He send them away? It is getting late, and obviously, it is impossible for us to feed this multitude."

In fact, according to Mark 6:35, the disciples actually came to tell Jesus to please send the people away before it got too late.

Jesus smiled and asked Philip, *Where can we buy some bread for these people to eat?* Apparently, Jesus didn't intend to send them away empty-handed.

The commentator quickly added, *He only said this to test Philip, He Himself knew exactly what He was going to do,* meaning that Jesus wasn't asking so that they could brainstorm and seek a solution to this perplexing situation. He was in complete control; the Bible says, *He knew what He wanted to do.*

Sometimes, God uses some situations to test our faith in Him, the sincerity of our love for Him and the extent of our obedience.

This is similar to what we have in today's First Reading. Elisha told his servant to serve twenty barley loaves and fresh grain to a hundred hefty men. The servant objected; Elisha insisted and eventually God's power was vindicated.

Philip was a rational being and a good mathematician, that was why he quickly told Jesus that feeding the crowd was rationally and naturally impossible. He had his grounds, three logical premises and a sound conclusion:

- Two hundred denarii are eight month's wages for a working man. They didn't have that kind of money.
- Even if they were able to raise two hundred denarii from the crowd, which supermarket in the wilderness would have bread for about 20,000 people.
- Even if they were lucky enough to find any, which was impossible anyway, the people would only get a bite, and a bite of bread wouldn't be sufficient for these hungry people.

Philip told Jesus "it is not possible at all"; a valid premise and a sound conclusion.

God is not limited by what we think; by our logic or sound reasoning. He is not bound by what the world says because for Him, nothing is impossible.

As this rational interaction was going on, the disciples sprang into action, asking people "do you have some bread?" Everyone was saying, "No", not at all, I forgot to buy some."

Andrew eventually found a boy who was willing to let go of his own lunch, (five Barley loaves and two tiny sardine-like fish). Let us pause and reflect here.....

Do you think that was the only boy with food in the crowd? It can't be the case; many hoarded their meals, but he was the only one who brought his out, not minding that he might go hungry, not minding that it was not good enough.

I have no idea why Andrew bothered to bring this to Jesus and he quickly defended his rationality by adding, *What is that between so many?*

Here lies the error in his judgement. Like Philip, he had passed judgement without considering the man standing before him.

Come to think of this, on a lighter note, if that bread and fish had got into the hands of some of us, it wouldn't have got to Jesus. We would have stayed somewhere and eaten it and come back to tell Jesus, "No one has anything, we didn't even get a single loaf of bread."

There is so much insincerity and deception in our world today. It is increasingly becoming more difficult to trust people.

Are we trustworthy? Are we honest? Are we reliable?

St. Paul tells us in the Second Reading to lead a life worthy of our vocation. A life of truth, justice, sincerity, self-lessness, gentleness and peace. Is this how we have been living?

So, Jesus stretched the faith of the disciples further. He said *make the people sit down.* I imagine what would have been going on in the minds of the disciples. I am sure they were reluctant to carry out this last order. They would have thought "why should we raise their hope for food when we don't have food to give them?

Remember; *He Himself knew exactly what He was going to do.* Jesus took the bread and what next? He gave thanks. After this, He took the fish and gave thanks also and the disciples began to share.

Ordinarily, I would end this sermon here, although there are still so many details to discuss. However, I want us to reflect on this act. Jesus had five barley loaves, and two fish for 20,000 people and yet He gave thanks.

Brethren; let us look at Jesus and look at ourselves. Do we realise how ungrateful we can be sometimes? We complain so much and so often. Many of us behave as if the problems of the whole world are on our shoulders.

Beloved in the Lord, think well; no matter what our condition in life, God has given us enough to be grateful for. Can we learn to be thankful even for our challenges because they also have their purpose in our life otherwise they wouldn't be there? 1 Thessalonians 5:18 says, *in all circumstances, give thanks, for this is the will of God in Christ Jesus for you.*

Let me quickly add this; gratitude when we are heart-broken and in need is evidence of deep faith. It causes confusion to the devil and it always attracts the blessings of God.

After giving thanks, they began to share the bread, and there was a miraculous multiplication. On that day, people ate and were satisfied. The Greek word is *enepleithesan* ('til their belly was full and could no longer take anything).

I am more interested in the boy who gave up his lunch. Oh, how great the happiness of this boy would have been. He gave to Jesus what Jesus used to feed the 20,000 strong crowd. I can hear him telling his mother, after the news has filled all ears and headlines in Galilee and Jerusalem. "Mum, it was my bread that Jesus blessed and used for the miracle." On his part, he must have eaten about ten loaves and five fish. He got back more than he gave.

The point I am making is that you can never lose what you give to God but what you can't offer to Jesus, you can never gain. Think about that.

Those who hid their own food could no longer eat it, it would have spoiled in their bags. Everybody ate and was abundantly satisfied. Jesus told the disciples to pack the rest, because our God is a God of sufficiency and abundance but not a God of wastage.

Remember, how this whole thing started, Philip said it was not possible to feed the crowd and now they had leftover food after feeding the crowd. Jesus turned to Philip and asked again, *Philip, is it possible to feed this crowd?* Philip said, *now I know that with you nothing is ever impossible.*

Jesus is smiling. He is looking at all of you listening to me now and saying, "having seen what I did with the crowds, do you believe that your case is also possible?"

What will your answer be?

*****

THE FOOD THAT LASTS

READING TEXTS:
EXODUS 16:2-4, 12-15;
PSALM 78:3, 4, 23-25;
EPHESIANS 4: 7, 20-24; JOHN 6: 4-35

An old woman fainted one day at mass during the Creed. Church members gathered around her and were vigorously praying for her. When she regained consciousness, she told them, "please, give me food, I am hungry."

In other words, "thanks for your prayers, but I fainted not because I was slain by the spirit but because I was hungry. I haven't had any food today."

Food is very important in a person's life. That is why one of the ways to attract anyone is to feed them. If our evangelisation is centred only on preaching, without a genuine concern for people's bodily needs, without a tangible action to help alleviate hunger and basic human needs, then the approach is lopsided.

In the First Reading, God fed about two and a half million people every day for forty years. This was to impress on them that their God cares for them and that He was sufficient to meet their needs. With this understanding, He could then draw them to a covenantal exclusive relationship with Himself.

In today's Gospel, we see people running after Jesus because He had fed them, with bread and fish. I can't blame the people, many of them had never known what it meant to eat well, never mind being satisfied and leaving some. They must have gathered all their family members, neighbours, friends and acquaintances to come to Jesus, perhaps in hope of another free meal.

At this time, the people would have been up to 35,000 in number. They looked for Jesus and they found Him because "those who diligently look for Him will find Him." Upon finding Him, they asked, *Rabbi, when did you come here?*

Instead of answering directly, Jesus moved to address their intention for looking for Him. He says, *I tell you most solemnly, you are not looking for me because you have seen the signs but because you had all the bread you wanted to eat.*

Brethren; let us pause and reflect here. This statement of Jesus carries a whole lot of weight.

We shall ask three questions here:

- Why do I do what I am doing?
- Why do I look for Jesus?
- Why do I follow those I am following?

I. *Why do I do what I am doing?*

Dear friends, God is interested not just in what we do, but why we do it? We may be charitable, friendly, hard-working and dutiful. People may praise our dedication and generosity, but ask yourself why are we doing all this?

Often, behind our seemingly kind deeds, is selfish interest. Jeremiah 17:10 tells us that the Lord searches the heart and probes the loins and He will give to everyone what his conduct and actions deserve.

II. *Why do I look for Jesus?*

Why am I in this Church? Why do I worship God? What is my intention for serving God? It's so funny that many of us are prompted not by "love but by loaves." We have seen instances of people who stop coming to Church because they lost someone dear to them, because they prayed for something and didn't get it. Can we say such people are serving God or that they want to be served by God?

Once God doesn't do for them what they wished for, then "to hell with God." Three things must objectively prompt us to serve God:

- Love for He who loves us first.
- Gratitude for His unmerited kindness.
- Desire for eternal happiness with Him for whom we are made.

III. *Why do you follow those you are following?*

Many of us really need to ask ourselves this fundamental question. Why am I following those I am following?

Food that lasts

Jesus gave the people a very powerful admonition that should re-echo in our ears and minds today. He said: *Do not work for food that cannot last...*

Dear friends, Jesus is saying something important to us. What do we waste our energies on? What do we waste our anxieties on? What are our predominant cares and worries? What are our aims in life? What are we labouring for?

Imagine how far people must have come from, just to fill their bellies. They would go that far just to eat bread. In pursuing things that are temporal, we often expend so much energy, time and labour without complaining.

I really wish these things would be relevant even after this world, but it is so sad, as all these will be worthless once we depart this sinful world.

Jesus says to us today, work for the food that lasts. I feel like opening the Bible now and reading this Psalm loud and clear: Psalm 49:0-12, 17-20.

Dear friends, what are we desperate about? What do we labour for? What are we pursuing in life?

Let me tell you the foods that last that we should seek:

- Seek to be intimate with our God.
- Seek to live good and holy lives.
- Seek to be a blessing to our generation.
- Seek to die a happy death .
- Seek a happy eternity.

Happy Sunday to you all.

*****

ELIJAH'S JOURNEY TO THE MOUNTAIN OF GOD

READING TEXTS:
1 KINGS 19:4-8; PSALM 34:2-9;
EPHESIANS 4:30-5:2;
JOHN 6:41-51

Dearly beloved in Christ, we thank God for His love upon us always and for the privilege to be in His presence today. Today is the Nineteenth Sunday in Ordinary Time, year B. Today I want to tell you about the Prophet of God named Elijah.

Elijah was a very great Prophet in the Old Testament. He was a prophet and wonderworker in the Northern Kingdom of Israel during the reign of Ahab (9th century BC). We can find his story in the first book of the Kings, chapters 17-19.

Elijah stood for God at a time when idolatry had become the celebrated religious practice. He opposed Baal, the Canaanite deity. He boldly announced God's curse on king Ahab for condoning idolatry and leading people astray from the true worship of God.

Just as his name suggests in Hebrew: אֵלִיָּהוּ, Eliyahu, meaning *my God is Yahu* (Yahweh), he declared for Yahweh and waged war against idolatry.

Elijah performed many miracles. For instance, he predicted drought and it happened; he blessed the widow of Zarephath, and her jar of flour and the jug of oil was not spent throughout the period of the famine. Elijah singlehandedly challenged 450 prophets of Baal and 400 prophets of Asherah to a contest at Mount Carmel. In that episode, Elijah called upon God and God sent fire from above to show that the God of Elijah is the true, living and capable God.

What a great man Elijah was. Even at the completion of his life, he was taken up *by a whirlwind*. Sirach 48:1-12 is a eulogy specially dedicated to this icon.

Why have we chosen to talk about Elijah today? Why not Nehemiah or Obadiah, Zechariah or Zephaniah or any of the Old Testament prophets? The reason is that the First Reading of today calls our attention to him.

The First Reading tells us of a shocking reality about Elijah. As courageous, powerful and privileged as Elijah was, Elijah had it so tough and rough that he begged God for death. I mean here we have a hero, a champion, a paradigmatic prophet who contemplated and desired death.

Why now? Elijah who was a prophet of God the Maker of earth and heaven, became a fugitive. The land of Israel, his God's land, was made hot and unlivable for him. He was threatened by a wicked woman, Jezebel, who had threatened him and sworn that she would stop at nothing to kill him. Elijah had trekked for many miles, he was so tired, he was hungry, he was depressed, and he begged God for death. He slept hoping to wake up across the bridge.

Unfortunately for him, God did not give what he asked for. God sent an angel to feed him miraculously, twice. He ate and when he recovered his strength, he stopped praying for death, he jumped up, shook his body, flexed his muscles and continued to the mountain of God.

What does God have for us this Sunday?

I. Elijah knew the truth, he stood for the truth; the truth was the uncommon opinion, it was not a popular notion. Many laughed at him, many murmured against him. Jezebel hated him; Ahab dug his pit. Elijah did not compromise, his God was Yahweh. It was a battle between the consensus of men and divine mandate.

   This is exactly what happened in today's Gospel. Jesus used food to attract the people to come and hear an important message. He was the bread of life that they needed. That is the simple but life-changing truth. To this, many grumbled, and many gathered against Him. Jesus didn't try to join them or cut down the truth to accommodate them.

   Dear friends, we often find ourselves in this kind of situation, when we are standing alone, or we are very few who are still standing for what is true, ideal, virtuous and godly. Do not compromise, do not be bent by public opinion, do not be swept away by what is democratic or popular. Live for the truth and die for it, even if that means living and dying alone.

II. As heroic and iconic as Elijah was, he met with a situation that caused him to beg for death. Death is better than a life of endless sorrow and unlimited misery. He said he could not continue. This is interesting, as it also happened to Moses; he also begged God for death (Numbers 11:15). We all know Job in the Bible; at the heart of his troubles, he wished he was never born (Job 3:1ff).

Maybe we are in that kind of situation now; we are tired of life; we are tired of everything. We are even tired of ourselves. We are already wishing for death. Maybe we are just depressed, and it seems our world has crumbled, and heaven has fallen upon us. Maybe we are here, and the devil is suggesting suicide to us or he is telling us that death is better than a miserable life.

Dear friends, I have a message of hope for you. It is simple but powerful. The Lord knows our plight, the Lord cares about us. We are not alone in our situation; even in the wilderness, God cares, in the land of slavery, He cares, in the fire, He cares, in the middle of the sea, He cares. It is only souls in hell that have eternally lost opportunities to enjoy His care.

Hear this, our condition is for a purpose and it is not our conclusion.

See how God treated Elijah. He prayed for death and hoped to wake among the deceased, but God gave him strength instead of death. Our case would be twice as terrible sometimes if God should take us at our word and grant us our passionate requests. But God who knows everything will always give us what we need even when it is not what we want.
(cf Matthew 7:9-11).

III. Let us see where Elijah was going today. He was going to Horeb, the mountain of God, to meet God (1

Kings 19:8). He was tired and God supplied what he needed to get to his destination.

Like Elijah, we are pilgrims in this world, on a long walk to see our God. The road is rough, narrow, tiring and uneasy. God knows this and so He has given us all we need for the journey; all we need to strengthen us.

For instance, the Word of God that we are listening to now is God's provision for us, a light on your path to God. Very soon, we shall eat "the bread of life" to strengthen our souls, to give us the strength to forge ahead and to win the battle of life, the battle especially against sin and all enemies of our salvation.

The bread of life will transform us into becoming He whom we receive. We have the sacrament of confession to lighten the burden of sins that can weary our souls; we have friends in heaven to assist us, just as the Angels woke Elijah and brought him food.

Dear friends, God has made enough provisions for us not to perish. If we perish, it's our choice and if we make that choice, it is woe.

Happy Sunday to you all.

*****

82

LIVING A LIFE OF WISDOM

READING TEXTS:
PROVERBS 9:1-6; PSALM 34,
EPHESIANS 5:15-20;
JOHN 6:51-58

In today's First Reading, wisdom is being presented to us as a royal and beautiful woman who has a beautiful palace with a dining hall, in which she organises a great feast. She, therefore, sent all her maids to call her guests.

Who are the guests? All who wish to possess wisdom, all who realise that they are ignorant and really desire to live good, responsible and meaningful lives.

The responsorial Psalm of today invites us to come and learn the true and wise way of life. The last stanza tells us about that meaningful life, it says;

- Guard your tongue against evil and your lips should refrain from deceit.
- Turn aside from evil and do good.
- Seek after peace and pursue it.

The Second Reading takes up this theme: *Look carefully, brethren, how you walk, not as unwise men but as wise, making the most of the time. Therefore, do not be foolish but understand what the will of the Lord is...*

St. Paul went ahead and added, *and do not get drunk with wine...*

St. Paul is here telling us that there are two kinds of lives; the life of wisdom and the life of foolishness.

In today's Gospel, we encounter Jesus who is wisdom incarnate, as He was teaching a sublime truth that reveals the wisdom of God. What is this truth?

He is the true bread which comes from heaven; His body is real food and His blood is real drink; His flesh and blood give life, and all who partake of them shall have eternal life.

His listeners couldn't relate with this because it takes divine wisdom to understand.

Today, dear friends, let us reflect on the wise life; that is, living a life of wisdom. I will just talk about five points on the life of wisdom.

I. *The life of wisdom consists of avoiding what can ruin us, our integrity, our reputation and destiny.*

The things many of us desire are the things that can destroy us. The things we pursue are the things that can bring us shame. A wise life is a life in which one desists from desiring, pursuing or enjoying what can ruin the soul. This is a life of self-denial and discipline; a life of careful reflection and proper use of freedom, when we don't have to blame our actions on the devil or beg for clemency when we should have avoided the act. It is the conscious choice to avoid what we will regret in the long run.

II. *The life of wisdom consists of wise use of resources.*

Many spend their money on things that are useless. Many spend money on what is injurious to their health and wellbeing. Many abandon legitimate financial responsibility to embrace financial irresponsibility.

This is a lack of financial wisdom. Many are in want, many run into heart-aching debts, many run into loss, because of lack of financial wisdom and discipline.

We need financial wisdom; we must learn to spend prudently, avoid meaningless and misguided spending on fanfares of vanity, ensure that there is provision for charity in our budget, donate to God's cause (Proverbs 3:9), bless someone with our finance and avoid incurring unnecessary debts.

III. *The life of wisdom consists of judicious use of time.*

Wisdom is reflected in the proper use of time. We are given time to find eternity. Do not waste time, do not lavish time in gossip or fruitless endeavours. Make meaningful use of time. Many waste their time away on social media. Social media has caused so much spiritual recession; devotion to Facebook, WhatsApp and Twitter has gradually weakened devotion to God and the things of God.

It is wise to use time to better our life, and spend time with our family, because our bond is time-bound and can elapse sooner than we think. Use time to do penance, to acquire virtues, to deepen knowledge, to multiply good works, to work for our salvation.

Time is most invaluable.

IV. *The life of wisdom is seen in the choice of friends.*

A wise person mingles with people who fear God, who are purpose-driven; people whose values are noble; people with vision and character.

A fool mingles with people who will destroy his mind, soul and body. He mingles with people who will introduce him to a culture of death and civilisation of evil.

Who are our companions? Who are those we mingle with? Our company influences our character and it will determine our destiny in life (Proverbs 13:20).

V. *The life of wisdom is seen in openness to God's Word and its joyful acceptance.*

A person who listens to God's Word, accepts it, obeys it and lives his life in accordance with it, is a wise person. The Word of God makes us wise (Psalm 119:98-100, 130).

In today's Gospel, some people reacted to the message of God because the wisdom therein exceeded the compass of their simple minds, and it offended their comfort. They couldn't abide by it and so they picked offence.

Picking offence at God's Word, being indifferent to it, not allowing it to touch, mould, renew and remould us, is not wisdom, and such attitude can only keep us confined to the domain of senselessness.

I end this reflection by reiterating the words of St. Paul in the Second Reading: *be very careful about the sort of lives you lead, like intelligent and not like senseless people.*

Happy Sunday to you all.

FREEDOM AT THE SERVICE OF TRUTH

READING TEXTS:
JOSHUA 24:1-2, 15-18; PSALM 34;
EPHESIANS 5:21-32;
JOHN 6:60-69

Dearly beloved in the Lord, today is the Twenty First Sunday in Ordinary time, year B. We thank God for the privilege of coming together in His presence. As we gather to worship today, may we experience His presence in a powerful, personal and profound manner.

Today's First Reading reveals an interplay between truth and freedom.

Joshua gathered the people of Israel to tell them the truth at Shechem. At this time, the Lord had settled them on the Canaanite soil. They now lived in peace and Joshua was already very old.

The people had been very unstable in their faithfulness to God. They were always too quick to deviate to idolatry.

Today, they needed to make a choice, a fundamental choice.

Two important points I want to present before us today.

1. A time comes when we must decide; we cannot escape making some decisions. A time comes when we decide what we want to do, how we want to live, whom we wish to be.

   Many of us have been struggling with some decisions, especially about our relationship with God. We want to serve God, we want to surrender to Jesus, we want to put an end to a particular way of living, to a particular way of earning a livelihood. However, we have been afraid, in doubt, uncertain, indecisive.

   Dear friends, the Lord is telling us to decide today. Many delay decisions until it became too late. The Lord is calling us to decide today but decide wisely.

2. We have the freedom to decide; the Lord doesn't force anyone, and He doesn't take away our freedom. We are free to decide what we want in life.

   We are free to decide to serve God or not to serve Him. We are free to decide how we want to live our lives. We are free to decide what we want in life.

   However, our freedom is relative because we shall also be responsible for our choices. Adam and Eve chose to disobey God and we know the consequences.

The last stanza of today's responsorial Psalm says;

> *evil brings death to the wicked; those who hate the good are doomed. The Lord reasons the souls of His servants. Those who hide in Him shall not be condemned.*

This means, we are free to choose evil, but we cannot choose an action and at the same time control/choose His consequence. Our freedom ends with the choice of action; it doesn't extend to the consequences.

The Second Reading of today tells us the truth about the family. Let us look at some of the points therein:

- Wives must surrender to their husband as head, just as the Church surrenders to Christ as her head.
- Husbands should love their wives as Jesus loved the Church and sacrificed Himself for her.

This is the truth about family life. We are free to decide today whether we want to obey it or not. We must all keep in mind that using our freedom to choose what is wrong is an abuse of freedom and for every use of freedom, there is accountability.

In the Gospel today, we are at the climax of Jesus' teaching on the bread of life. Today was the day of decision. He had presented the truth to them and so they had to decide whether to freely accept or not. He would not force anyone, not even His disciples.

Many chose to be angry; they protested and refused to believe this particular doctrine but then they remained with Him.

Some could not cope, "He is delaying the bread that brought us here and He is here speaking 'rubbish'," and so, many left.

He even asked His disciples if they wanted to leave. It was not by force.

We also have the freedom to accept the truth or not. What then is our response to the truth? What is our response when we are confronted with the truth about our lives, when we are confronted with the truth that disturbs our preferences?

Let's analyse how many of us respond:

- Many respond with gestures (affirmative nod, shaking the head, tears, a deep sigh etc.), but then they continue in the way of error and sin.
- Many respond by justifying why they should continue in error.
- Many get angry at the one who tells the truth (read Jeremiah chapter 42 to chapter 43).
- Many avoid the one who tells them the truth (read 1 Kings 22; Ahab always avoided Micaiah son of Imlah).
- Some will look for a way to disrepute the one who claims to be the voice of truth. This is what the enemies of the Church are trying to do against the Church; making all efforts to discredit the Church because of the values she upholds and the truth she stands for.

For standing against abortion, contraceptives, euthanasia, homosexuality, invitro-fertilization, divorce etc., the secular world, instead of accepting the truth is seeking to destroy the integrity and moral probity of the Church, so that once this is destroyed, the Church will lose stamina and the confidence to preach the truth.

This is also an attitude to the truth; this represents a way of using our freedom. However, the truth remains the truth and we shall be judged according to how we use our freedom to accept or reject the truth.

Happy Sunday to you all.

WORTHLESS WORSHIP

READING TEXTS:
DEUTERONOMY 4:1-2, 6-8;
PSALM 15; JAMES 1:17-27;
MARK 7:1-23

Today is the Twenty Second Sunday in Ordinary time, year B. We praise the name of the Lord for this assembly of joy and may God draw us closer to Himself and may His light penetrate every darkness in our hearts.

In the First Reading today, Moses admonished the people to faithfully keep the commandments of God. Keeping the commandments would do three things for them:

- It would demonstrate their wisdom (as we have also in Psalm 119:98-100).
- It would make them distinct and different from other nations around.
- It would not destroy their freedom but strengthen it. Obedience to God's laws doesn't deprive us of our freedom but testifies that we are free. True freedom is in the ability to obey what is right and just.

The Psalm of today tells us that obedience to God's laws will do two things for us:

- It will better our relationship with one another.
- It will give us access to God's presence.

In the Second Reading, St. James tells us the essence of true religion, namely:

- To obey God's Word and not just listen and remain unchanged.
- To be charitable to the vulnerable, the needy and those at the margins of society.

In today's Gospel, we see Jesus trying to teach us the true meaning and essence of religion. The Pharisees were angry that the disciples did not follow the ritual purification of hands before eating. Jesus saw something wrong with the disposition of the Pharisees, namely that they emphasised the externality without paying attention to what was inward.

Of what use is washing the body when the heart is dirty and filthy. Jesus went ahead to quote the prophecy of Isaiah which should also make us reflect:

> *This people honours me only with lip-service, while their hearts are far from me. The worship they offer me is worthless...*

The Message of Today

Dear friends in Christ, all the readings of today should spur us into reflection.

What is true religion? What makes worship worthless? How are we supposed to worship God and be acceptable to Him?

I shall be preaching on: Four symptoms of a worthless religion.

I. A *religion that is merely external, without inward transformation.*

Jesus gave a good analogy. This kind of religious attitude is like washing the outside of the dish without washing the inside. Religion is supposed to wash us from within; to wash the filth in us; the wickedness, impurity, defilement and sinfulness in our hearts.

Many people today are so religious, saying prayers, observing practices and devotions, faithful to postures, gestures, and religious observances, but their hearts are perverted, crooked and wicked. This is a worthless religion.

The Pharisees typified this category very well. They carried the laws about, praying in the marketplaces, studying the law in open ceremonies, observing the "rubrics" of worship but then their hearts were full of envy, pride, evil intent and thought (for instance John 12:9-11).

Religion is principally to clean the heart, and all those external rites will make sense when they proceed forth from a renewed heart.

II. *Religion without obedience.*

This is what Moses told the people in today's First Reading. They must obey God's commandments. This is what St. James says in the Second Reading as well; we must listen to God and obey Him.

If we claim to worship God but we live in disobedience to His will, His laws and decrees, then it is worthless worship. 1 Samuel 15:22: ...*surely to obey is better than sacrifice, and to heed than the fat of rams.*

Anyone who claims to worship God but lives his life in disobedience to God's commandments, is showing worthless worship.

III. *Religion without character.*

Religion ought to help us to become better people; to become more responsible. It converts us from within and transforms our character. We can relate better with others and manifest godly conduct and disposition.

A religion that isolates us from others and makes it impossible for us to relate with others and for others to be able to relate well with us, is corrupt and worthless.

IV. *Religion without mercy and love.*

This is the main case that St. James advanced. Worshipping God should form us to be more merciful, more tolerant, more compassionate and loving to others. These are attributes of God that closeness to God should form in us. If we claim to be close to God and love and mercy for others are not dominant in our traits, our life calls for examination.

If despite our piety, we still find it simple and compatible to be wicked, to nurture hatred and desire for revenge, if we can still wish harm and misery for others, if the suffering of a particular person or people brings us joy, if we can be indifferent to people's cry for pardon and mercy, then our worship may be many miles from what God accepts.

CARING FOR THE POOR

READING TEXTS:
ISAIAH 35:4-7;
PSALM 146; JAMES 2:1-5;
MARK 7:31-37

There are some things we do in life, that we enjoy doing at the time, but their eventual effects on us are usually disastrous.

Today, I want to mention five of such things. These five misconducts can result in misfortune.

- Theft.
- To betray/hurt someone who trusts us so much.
- To maltreat or disrespect one's parents.
- To treat God's ministers with scorn or contempt.
- To oppress, disregard or be unjust to the vulnerable (children, aged, poor, needy, physically challenged, helpless widow, defenceless orphan etc.).

I want to make this fifth point my gateway to today's reflection. Dear friends, there is a tendency in many of us, that God is calling us today to correct. This is the tendency to treat some people with honour and to treat others with scorn, according to their state and condition in life.

Often, we are tempted to treat with disrespect those we call poor, those who can't dare us, those we are stronger than, those we think have nothing to offer us, those we think nature has humiliated, those who have noticeable defects, those we call ugly, those who are at the lower margins of social status, those we think we are better than.

We then treat with honour, respect and sometimes even begin to worship, wealthy, powerful and connected people, those we believe have what we lack, those to whom we look up to for assistance, those we think are better than us, those who can displace us, those we call pretty etc.

The Lord is calling us today to a change of attitude.

Three points we must keep in mind:

- Those we think are useless and helpless are specially loved by God. In Jesus' manifesto, you see that there is a preferential option for them (Luke 4:18-19).
- Our attitude to them can either gain us blessings or curse. They are very sure means of obtaining blessings from God (Proverbs 19:17).
- Only God knows tomorrow. Those we term unfortunate today may become our benefactors tomorrow; those we think are blessed today may become miserable tomorrow (remember Luke 16:19-31- Lazarus and the rich man).

With this in mind, we can now go through the readings.

The First Reading of today is a prophecy of hope for the people of God in exile. They were poor, miserable, banished and humiliated in the land of Babylon, but then the Lord through the Prophet Isaiah, showed that He cared for them, that they were His people whom He loved, and that He was coming soon to liberate and restore them. Though poor and miserable, they were loved by God.

The Psalmist of today also proclaims God's love for the oppressed, hungry, prisoners, the blind, the stranger, the widow and orphan.

The Second Reading of today tells us to avoid all forms of discrimination between classes of people. St. James sternly warns against treating the rich with respect and the poor with disdain. He ends by telling us that the poor have a special place in the heart of God.

In today's Gospel, we have an encounter between Jesus and a man who is deaf and has a speech impediment; the kind of man most of us would not want to have anything to do with.

Before I proceed further, let us pause and do two things:

1. Let us imagine how it is to be deaf and dumb. Imagine that you see or think of something and you are unable to express it in words or someone says something, and people are laughing, and you are just there looking because you can't hear. It is like the person is cut off from life; he can only see but can't say or hear. It's terrible.
2. Let us thank God for the gift of our senses and their functioning. Let us pray that the Lord will preserve our senses and we pray for those whose senses are malfunctioning; may they experience the loving kindness of God.

Back to the discussion; look at the attention that Jesus gave to this man. He took him aside, to give him special attention and to teach us from His example, to do good without seeking glory and people's applause.

He put His fingers into his ears as if to remove that which had blocked his ears and touched his tongue with spittle to loosen that which had tied his tongue. He looked up to heaven and sighed, looking up to heaven to give the Father praise for what He was about to do.

By sighing, He expressed His pity for the miseries of human life and His sympathy for the afflicted in their afflictions.

He said to him "*Ephphatha*," which is "be opened." Jesus spoke with authority, and power went with His words. These are the same words used at baptism, to impress on us that internal impediments of the mind are removed by the Spirit of Christ, just as those bodily impediments were removed by the power of His Word.

I believe many of us here need this kind of miracle as well. We need God to open our minds and hearts as He did to Lydia (Acts 16:14) so that we may understand, accept and treasure His words.

We need God to open our ears so that we can hear the promptings of the Holy Spirit.

We need God to touch and open our mouth and cure us of all bad words, lies, curse and immodest talk, so that we may begin to use our tongues to proclaim His goodness and speak what glorifies Him.

Dear friends, let us thank God for His words and make up our minds today to begin to love, to care for, to be kind to and treat with respect all those whom society relegates to the margin.

*****

Twenty Fourth Sunday In Ordinary Time

PROOF OF A LIVING FAITH

READING TEXTS:
ISAIAH 50:5-9;
PSALM 115; JAMES 2:14-18;
MARK 8:27-35

Today is the Twenty Fourth Sunday in Ordinary time, year B. We are happy to be in the presence of the Lord.

Psalm 65:4:
> *happy are those whom you choose and bring near to be in your court. We shall be satisfied with the goodness of your house, of your holy temple.*

As we have come today, may we be satisfied with the blessings that flow from His presence.

Today, I shall be preaching on what I titled: *Proof of Living Faith.*

One of the problems we have in Christianity today is that many of us claim to be believers, but we have no proof. We claim to be people of faith but there is no concrete evidence.

In our world today, where there is so much deception, we really need proof, clear evidence that someone is whom he/she claims to be.

St. James tells us in today's Second Reading that our works are the proof that we have living faith; that is to say, every claim of faith without the evidence of good works is dead.

This morning let us examine five kinds of work which testify and serve as proof that we have a faith that is alive.

I. *Kindness to the needy*

St. James cites an instance here. A brother/sister comes to us hungry and in need of clothes. We simply pray, quote some Bible verses and dismiss him/her in peace according to a proper liturgical formula. He says such faith is dead.

Faith is expressed in genuine concern and kindness to the needy. Whether the person deserves it or not is not the point; whether the person has been kind to us in times past is not the issue. True and living faith moves us to show sincere kindness to people.

Today, we see this kind of faith in people who have dedicated themselves or a huge chunk of their resources to helping the needy. This is a lively faith animated by charity.

II. *Working for peace*

Evidence of faith is a passion for peace and reconciliation. True faith is demonstrated by avoiding what can destroy peace and seeking to establish peace where it is broken or threatened.

Interestingly and sadly though, many of us believers are agents of division and disunity. We are mischief-makers; we claim to serve a God of peace while our conduct and actions show that we do not belong to the kingdom of peace.

We fuel the embers of crises, stir the waters of trouble, we are at the forefront in advancing family crises. Instead of being peacemakers, we wage war against peace and reconciliation. This is clear proof that we do not believe in the God of peace.

III. *Response/Disposition to our cross*

In the Gospel, Jesus spoke to the disciples about the cross ahead of Him, and His willingness to accept it. Our disposition in moments of crises, our reactions when things go wrong, our attitude when we do not get what we pray for from God, when we feel disappointed, when our crosses are placed on our shoulders, these are the tests of the genuineness of faith.

In the Gospel, Jesus tells us: *if anyone wants to be a follower of mine, let him renounce himself and take up his cross and follow me.*

St. Paul demonstrated the firmness of his faith amid his cross when he says in Romans 8:35-39 that nothing in this world can ever and will ever separate him from the love of God, not even his crosses. This is proof of living faith.

IV. *Reaction to those who bear us ill*

This is one of the greatest proofs of living and true faith; the way we react to those who offend us, those who malign us, those who embarrass us, those who betray us, those who after acting cruelly to us come back to ask for mercy and clemency.

The suffering servant of God in today's First Reading epitomises this very well. He didn't repay evil with evil, violence with violence, wickedness for wickedness; he only trusted in God to give his assailants what they deserved. This is proof of faith.

It is a sign of living faith when we do not allow people to force us to nurture hatred, enmity and bitterness, when we love the unlovable and forgive the unforgivable, when we overlook faults and enjoy an uninterrupted relationship with our God.

V. *Trust/calmness that God is in charge*

In life, there are just too many things that can evoke worries and anxieties and in fact, we are being tempted to become despondent, depressed, sad and heartbroken in the face of the challenges before us.

There are many reasons why we should ask, "how can I?", "how will I?", "why me?" Evidence of living faith is learning to trust in God that it is well, that God is in charge of everything, that God's will shall prevail, and that God is wiser than us.

This is the kind of faith that Paul demonstrated amid the storm in Acts 27:21-25. Trusting in God's power and love and being calm in the midst of the storm, great expectation, severe risk and uncertainties, is proof of living faith.

I end with Psalm 46:1-3, 7.

*****

WATCH YOUR DESIRES

READING TEXTS:
WISDOM 2:12, 17-20;
PSALM 54; JAMES 3:16-4:3;
MARK 9:30-37

Dearly beloved in the Lord, today is the Twenty Fifth Sunday in Ordinary Time, year B. The year is gradually drawing to a close. May we be blessed because we have come to be with the Lord today.

Today, I want to preach on what I have titled: *Watch Your Desires.*

In economics, we are told that human wants are insatiable. Then, a distinction is made between wants and needs.

Human wants are the things that the human mind desires. Human desires may be good or bad. Many times, the human person desires the things that are injurious to the soul, things that can endanger the salvation of the human person, the things that will violate our neighbours' freedom, rights and peace. Often, we desire what God has given to our neighbour.

What are the desires that sometimes occupy our minds?

- A property belonging to another. Ahab typified this when he became restive because of Naboth's vineyard (1 Kings 21).
- We often desire positions of power and offices that accord us some authority. Absalom is a case study here.
- We often desire earthly riches/wealth. We fantasise on the comfort it brings and the control we shall have on people, things and events.
- We often desire another person's wife, husband or even friend. David paradigmatised this in his desire for Bathsheba, the wife of Uriah (2 Samuel 11), Herod who "bracketed" his brother's wife is another case on point (Mark 6:17).
- Many people desire fame and recognition.

Most of these desires pose danger to our souls and the wellbeing of others. However, the danger is not just in our desires, but also in how we pursue them.

Let me identify five common, terrible ways we pursue our desires:

- We kill our opponents or anyone who tries to be a stumbling block.
- Many steal or illegitimately claim or hold on to what belongs to another.
- Many blackmail and tarnish the reputation of another to get their desired favour.
- Many join unchristian confraternities in a bid to get something they are ambitious about.
- Many people compromise their faith, subdue their consciences and by so doing, deny Christ in order to obtain a ticket to the top. Some Christians have become Muslims to secure political office and post.

Dear friends, the three readings of today serve as critical warnings to us all.

The First Reading tells us about the plot against the unsuspecting innocent. The innocent was an obstacle to them achieving their evil ambition and from having rest in their wickedness.

As such, they wanted to kill him. This is how far ambition can degenerate to wickedness.

Three important points from St. James today:

- Wherever jealousy and ambition co-exist, we find all forms of wickedness and disharmony.
- The wisdom from above is reflected in contentment, peace and charity to others.
- Our inordinate desires are the reasons we break faith with one another and act uncharitably to one another.

We see in today's Gospel how the disciples were also almost planting the seed of division through ambition; a seed that would have eventually grown to be an atomic plant of destruction.

Jesus was talking about His passion and redemptive death, yet the disciples were more concerned about power and who would control the rest of the apostles.

It was a heated debate. The disciples who thought themselves worthy came with their manifestos for the campaign.

If Jesus had not intervened and they were left to follow that simple, innocent-seeming inquiry "who is the greatest?", maybe schism and mutual suspicion would have ruined that company, as it has ruined many friends, homes and families.

My dear friends, let us keep these five things in mind:

- Let us be contented in life and thank God for and appreciate what we have. We should not be restive over what is not ours.
- Let us learn to discipline our minds and desires. We must not have everything we desire.
- We should not ever ruin, tarnish or kill anyone to step up in life. We should not use people to advance and achieve our selfish intentions. We should watch how we pursue our desires.
- We should not lose our salvation to gain the whole world or something in the world. (Mark 8:36). Give up today any desire that can ruin our soul.
- Let us be careful what we do to others when we need to fulfil an ambition. Remember nemesis; remember that God is all-seeing, and He is a just judge. Remember that whatever goes around comes around and remember that He will give to everyone what his conduct and actions deserve.

*****

WAGE AGAINST
ENVY

READING TEXTS:
NUMBERS 11:25-29;
PSALM 19; JAMES 5:1-6;
MARK 9:38-48

Astory was told about a holy man and his mother. According to human judgement, the mother was a pious woman, and everybody expected her to enter heaven. After her death, she was sent to purgatory. She had a weakness that must be purified; there was still some "selfishness" in her conduct. Some years after, her son died, and he was so surprised to know his mother didn't make heaven directly. He was also surprised to know that since her death, she was still in purgatory. So, the son implored God to have mercy on his mother, and God told the son that his mother wasn't ready for heaven yet. The son begged and begged, and God decided to test the woman.

An angel was sent to throw a rope down to her so that she could climb out of purgatory to heaven using the rope. When she saw the rope, she was happy and started to climb up. She had almost got out of purgatory, when she looked back and saw some other suffering souls holding onto the rope and climbing with her. She became furious and used her leg to hit them to go back. God now told the son, "Can you see your mother? You see that she's not yet rid of her self-centredness and her envy of others." The Angel then released the rope and she fell back into purgatory.

The Christian life is a life of constant struggles against some inclinations in us that are natural but are inconsistent with the life of grace we are called to live.

I will mention just five of those tendencies and focus on one.

I. *Pride:* The tendency to exaggerate our relevance and achievement and look down on others. This is what St. James condemned in the Second Reading (pride and insensitivity of the rich).

II. *Lust:* Inordinate desires of the flesh.

III. *Anger:* The inclination to be quick to harshly react to provocation.

IV. *Revenge:* The tendency not to let go of hurt and to wish harm to those who trespass against us.

V. *Envy:* The tendency to be distressed, to be angry or feel insecure because of something good happening in the life of another.

This morning, I want to focus on this tendency called envy.

In today's First Reading, Joshua was angry that Eldad and Medad, who were outside the tent, prophesied in the camp.

Joshua was angry and worried that these two also received the gift of prophecy. Moses answered him: *are you jealous for my sake? Would that all...were prophets...*

A similar thing happened in today's Gospel; let us see the wider context. The disciples of Jesus had just returned from a mission. They had cast out demons and preached in Christ's name. Everybody was talking about them; their power, their supernatural grace. Jesus Himself praised them. They were really happy, and they felt honoured.

However, they were unhappy to hear that another man, who was not a disciple was doing something similar and so they queried him and gave him a strict warning to go and do something else and leave that extraordinary deed to them. Why should he share in their glory? They expected Jesus to affirm their deeds, but He corrected their error.

Let me mention five indications/symptoms of the spiritual malady called envy:

1. When we feel threatened and insecure because something good is happening to someone else.
2. When we begin to announce to the world (most times with exaggeration), how we have been part of or instrumental to someone else's success. Sometimes we even expect to be worshipped because we played a part in someone's success.
3. When we begin to feel God is unkind to us and kind to others. When we think God is cheating us or robbing us to bless others. When we begin to calculate that someone's blessings ought to have been our lot. When we think we are the one who deserved what another person got.
4. When we begin to always find fault in someone whom others appreciate. When we begin to find it difficult to appreciate others and see something good in them.

109

5. When we always feel we must be the ones at the centre of attention and attraction. It's either us or no one else. There is a confluence between envy and self-centredness. It's an iron link.

Dear friends, God doesn't want us to be envious of His blessings to others. Let us kill in us the tendency to do anything to stop others who are more preferred to us. If we don't kill the tendency, it will ruin us. Remember Miriam and Aaron (Numbers 12:1-16).

Also read 1 Peter 2:1, James 3:16, Job 5:2.

Envy can push us to act wickedly, to be uncharitable to others or judge them harshly because of God's goodness to them. Remember Saul and David (1 Samuel 18:7; 29:5).

When we allow envy to rule us, we start fighting with God and protesting His goodness to others. For instance, the Jews against Paul (Acts 13:45), or the brothers of Joseph against him.

There's something in us that protests when others are being preferred to us, but that thing belongs to the old self, not the new self which a child of God must assume.

Let us all wage war against envy and enjoy interrupted peace and grace.

Happy Sunday to you and God bless.

*****

THE FAMILY: AN INDICATION OF GOD'S SENSITIVE LOVE

READING TEXTS:
GENESIS 2:18-24;
PSALM 128; HEBREWS 2:9-11;
MARK 10:2-16

For some days now we have been reading about the experience of Job. Job was suddenly plunged into an inexplicable abyss of deep misery. It became unbearable at some point and so he began to question God's love, care and power. Eventually, God answered Job and he (Job) immediately repented of his protest. After everything, the Lord restored the fortunes of Job a hundredfold.

The overriding lesson for us is that even in our "Job-like" experiences, God never stops loving and caring for us.

The readings of today, whilst they draw our attention to the sanctity of marriage, also vividly convey to us the message of God's love, care and sensitivity to human needs.

In today's First Reading, we encounter a God who loves humankind, who is always thinking about our wellbeing and who confers so much dignity on us.

God took note of the loneliness of Adam; isn't it consoling to know that God is taking note of our plight? God fashioned a suitable Helper for Adam. God doesn't just take note, He is also interested in helping us. He even gave man the honour of naming all He (God) created. Who told us, "you are a non-entity?" Before our God, we are all important and dignified.

From the First Reading, we are made to understand that God created family for the good and happiness of humankind. Eve was created to complete Adam, to be a suitable helper and a befitting companion.

The Gospel of today also reiterates the dignity and sanctity of family life. God created family as a society of love for the happiness of humankind. The Gospel went further to define family as a permanent union that is indissoluble and exclusive between a man and a woman.

Today, I wish to just draw five quick points for us to ponder on:

I.   *The first essence of marriage is companionship.*

This means that a wife and her husband must be good friends, they must communicate well, share love and life and help each other to grow in every positive aspect of life. Is this how our family is? Anything different from this is a deviation from divine intention.

II. *The second purpose of marriage is procreation and the formation of offspring.*

In marriage, have we been open to a new life or have we been standing against new life through abortion and contraceptives? The second stanza of today's Psalm says: *your children like shoots of the olive...* Is this the kind of children we have or are ours like a "thorn-bush" or un-pruned weed? Whose fault is that? Maybe God's fault, who tested us with the gifts of children?

III. *Marriage is a permanent union.*

It means that there is no provision for divorce (Malachi 2:16). Divorce is not just a formal, definitive and irrecon-cilable separation, but when a man and a woman stay together without living in love, openness, trust, peace and happiness, there is already a subtle divorce. Man and wife, are you together in love or divorced at heart?

IV. *Marriage is between a man and a woman.*

This comes with a lot of implications. I know many people will be uncomfortable with what I am about to say here, but I must preach the truth with conviction in and out of season, acceptable or otherwise because, in the long run, I will be accountable to God.

Marriage is never between a man and man, a woman and a woman, a man and many women, a woman and many men, a human being and a pet. As such all forms of perversion, homosexuality, lesbianism, bestiality, infidel-ity, even though they may be legal, are immoral and represent man's attempt to dare God.

Let us not wait to be punished before we repent. We are principally governed by God's law and we obey the state's laws in as much as they don't contravene God's laws.

V. *Whatever God has united man must not divide.*

Let us all be careful not to become an agent of the

destruction of marriage. Young ladies do not destroy people's homes by illicit affairs with married men. A man without self-control and discipline is not worthy of being called a man. Men, please be "manly", put your drive under check and don't become agents of destruction by wooing and lusting after another man's wife, remember the 9th commandment (Exodus 20:17).

Man and wife, the irresponsibility of a partner doesn't justify or become a license for the immorality of the other partner.

In-laws keep in mind; you must not be home-breakers. Home breakers are agents of the devil. Respect people's homes and keep a safe and dignifying distance. Respect the family's freedom and do not bring tension to a peaceful home.

To those widowed or experiencing marriage as a heavy cross, the Church unites with you in your pain. Keep in mind that God is also concerned about you and He loves and cares for you.

However, do not presume that God will understand if under the excuse of your state you committed the sin of impurity and sexual immorality. Remember that only the pure of heart will see God (Matthew 5:8). Unite your cross with that of Jesus, who as we have heard in the Second Reading, accepted suffering and death for us all.

May God bless our homes and make them a model of a redeemed family. May God bless our children and make them like shoots of the olive. May God bless the souls of the departed and grant them eternal rest 'til we meet again in joy and happiness forever.

*****

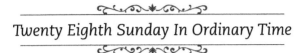

A MEDITATION ON DIVINE WISDOM

READING TEXTS:
WISDOM 7:7-11; PSALM 90;
HEBREWS 4:12-13,
MARK 10:17-30

There are three things I usually love meditating upon. They are three things that we need most in our lives. They are Grace, Mercy and Divine Wisdom.

Today, I shall be preaching on Divine Wisdom.

Divine Wisdom is that gift from God which enables us to make good choices in life, to live rightly, to enjoy our relationship with God, to coordinate our temporal affairs properly and be focused on our eternity.

The First Reading of today is in praise of Wisdom. The author is telling us at least two things:

- Wisdom is invaluable. It is to be desired and esteemed more than riches, power, gold, silver, health and beauty.
- Wisdom can be received through prayers.

The Gospel of today gives us at least five expressions/ indications of wisdom.

I.   *Wisdom consists in being concerned about our eternity.*

A young man ran to Jesus, knelt and asked: *What must I do to inherit eternal life?* Many people are concerned today about every other thing except eternal life. People are concerned about pleasure, fun, beauty, technology, music, sport, relationships, knowledge and fame.

We shall soon find out that coming to life is the greatest misfortune if it is not crowned with a happy eternity. Did you not hear the Psalmist of today? Make us know the shortness of our life, that we may gain wisdom of heart?

II.   *Wisdom consists in humility.*

The young man addressed Jesus as *Good master*, but Jesus replied, *no one is good except God alone.* We all know that Jesus is God, but that response is a demonstration of humility. Learning to give glory to God and being discreet about our own merits, goodness and achievement is wisdom. Pride is a confirmed symptom of foolishness.

III. *Wisdom consists in keeping God's commandments.*

Many people wrongly believe that wisdom and freedom are in living according to one's desire and pleasure, living wild and unmortified lives. Jesus is telling us today that wisdom is in mortification, a life of self-discipline and self-denial. Wisdom is not in obedience to one's carnal desires and dictates, but in submission to God's commandments.

This is where the Second Reading comes in. Wisdom is in living our lives according to the principles and dictates of God's Word. When we allow the Word of God to dictate and shape our lives, we become wiser than our peers (Psalm 119:98-100).

IV. *Wisdom is in detachment.*

Many of us are so attached to many things, and this attachment becomes a distraction to our relationship with God. Attachment to earthly goods and relationships (family and friends) is one of the things that make dying difficult.

Attachment to riches became the obstacle of this young man; he could not let go of his riches, and then he made the wrong choice. He chose earthly fortune and abandoned the eternal fortune of heaven and by that singular choice, he chose foolishness and misfortune.

Peter at the other end, represents the wisdom of detachment. He says, *we have left everything and followed you* (*emeis apheikamen panta kai ekoloutheikamen soi*).

Dear friends, what are we over-attached to? What is competing with the love of God and heaven in our lives? Today is the day to address it. Are we aware that one day we will be forced to detach from these things?

Have we not heard from the Scriptures that if our right eye or right hand will cause us to sin and lose heaven, cut them off (Matthew 5:29-30), and in another place, Scripture says blessed are the poor in Spirit for theirs is the kingdom of heaven? (Matthew 5:3)

V. *Wisdom consists in taking care of the poor.*

Did Jesus exhort the young man of today to sell all he had and build a supermarket or a coffee shop? Did Jesus tell him to invest the money or get a fish and chip store? No!

Jesus told him to go and take care of the poor. This is the most dignifying and lucrative business investment; the profit is eternal.

Dear friends, look around you, look behind you, look beside you. Even here in England, people are hungry and poor. There is so much poverty in our world today. What you give your pet dog to eat and the care you show them, are what some people somewhere need to be alive and happy again.

When you take care of the poor, you become a friend of God, and you are also storing up treasures and establishing friendships for yourself in heaven. In this, there is great wisdom.

Lord Jesus save us from a life of foolishness that leads to regret. Give us understanding and wisdom. Amen.

*****

THE REQUEST OF JAMES AND JOHN

READING TEXTS:
ISAIAH 53:10-11; PSALM 33;
HEBREWS 4:14-16;
MARK 10:35-45

One of the greatest tests to our faith is when we are in desperate need and we call on God in prayers, but we do not receive what we have prayed for. It feels like God is wicked, insensitive or even non-existent. Then sometimes we are tempted to ask, "what is the benefit of being a child of God if God deals with me this way?"

I have had my fair share of this test. Today, I want to recant the case of a woman (I call her Deborah here but that's not the real name) who lost her husband in a car crash after five years of marriage. Luckily she had a son (Kelvin, again not the real name) whom she loved so much. This was a very devout and dedicated woman. Unfortunately, her son who was 15 years old, and full of life, faith and promises, was diagnosed with a deadly heart disease. We prayed and prayed. I fasted and did several novenas, offered Masses but eventually the boy died.

It was a deep pain in her heart and a very difficult test on our faith too. Then, Deborah's sister had some complications after delivery of her child and was in a coma for two days. When she recovered, she told us of her experience. She had seen Kelvin, her sister's son. He was dressed in shining white and was in inexpressible happiness. His face was so bright, and his countenance was like an angel; he was in great glory and peace.

Deborah's sister was begging to follow him, but he was smiling and waving her to go back and then she woke. She woke in tears because she wanted to be where Kelvin was.

Her testimony gave us some consolation and strengthened our faith. We were praying that God should restore Kelvin but it pleased God more out of His love and wisdom, to call Kelvin to happiness, where there will be no more sickness and risk of losing heaven.

Sometimes we ask God to grant a particular favour, to remove a particular pain and sickness, to end an undesired phenomenon, but God acts differently.

When John the Baptist was in prison, his disciples prayed and fasted for him to be released but he was beheaded. Well, he was released but without his head.

In today's Gospel, James and John came to Jesus with their request; well, it doesn't sound like a request, more like a command. They requested Jesus to grant them a place of honour in his Kingdom. They wanted to be next in command to Him. This request was so important to them because they knew once Jesus died, they stood no chance among the disciples again.

There was already an ongoing underground campaign and the names of John and James never appeared among the probable candidates, even though they were among the earliest disciples to be called.

We read in Matthew 7:7, Jesus said, *ask and you will receive.* James and John asked today, and they didn't receive. Yes, they asked in ignorance; they were not properly motivated; they asked for the wrong thing. What they asked for contradicted God's will and so Jesus didn't oblige them. They felt the way we often feel when we do not receive what we ask for. They asked for seats of glory, they got a chalice of suffering.

Dear friends, faith is not just getting what we ask for, but trusting in God's power and love to give us what is good for us and a joyful acceptance of God's will even if it contradicts our desires.

Relegation, pains, sickness, sufferings, death, difficulties and hardships are not what we ordinarily wish or desire for ourselves but then, they often have a place in God's eternal designs of love for us.

The opening line of today's First Reading affirms this: *the Lord has been pleased to crush his servant with suffering* and the last line says, *By his sufferings shall my servant justify many...*

The Second Reading tells us that even Jesus our high priest, went through temptations and suffering. In the garden of Gethsemane, He also prayed that the cup of sufferings pass Him by, but He had to accept it. It was this same cup that Jesus told James and John to prepare for. Prestige and power are not an integral part of the discipleship package, but suffering is.

For the other disciples who were indignant because of the request of James and John, thank God Jesus intervened or who knows what would have happened afterwards. Maybe the other disciples would have conspired to poison or expel James and John. Maybe Matthew would have left the group out of frustration and Simon Peter would have been disqualified for lack of education. Judas probably would have become the head of the college since as the treasurer, he had the financial strength and cleverness.

The Gospel would have taken a different twist. Jesus taught them the same lesson as He is teaching you and me today. Following Christ doesn't mean being a victor all the time, getting what we want in prayers all the time or being in control, wielding power and influence and gaining recognition.

It is about:

- Accepting God's will even when it doesn't correspond with our will.
- It is about humility and willingness to serve others.
- It is about bearing suffering patiently without losing faith in God.

*****

THE ENCOUNTER BETWEEN JESUS AND BARTIMAEUS

READING TEXTS:
JEREMIAH 31:7-9, PSALM 126,
HEBREWS 5:1-6,
MARK 10:46-52

In the Gospel of today, we have a very touching story of the encounter between Jesus and Bartimaeus. It is not just the story of Bartimaeus but our own stories.

I shall divide the homily into two:

- The plight of Bartimaeus.
- The Grace of Bartimaeus.

I. *The Plight of Bartimaeus*

Bartimaeus had three observable misfortunes:

- *He was blind:* He could not behold the beauty of flowers, the brightness of stars, the smiles of a child. At night when he closed his eyes and in the morning when he opened them again, there was utter darkness. What a pity, we may say.

- *He was a beggar:* One may have a defect and yet be born in an affluent home and be cared for. Bartimaeus didn't have this "make-up"; he was begging for food and "pennies" to survive.
- *At the roadside of a cursed town:* He was begging at the roadside of a cursed town.
  (Joshua 6:26).

Ironically, Bartimaeus had a very good name; his name Bar-Timaeus means "Son of honour." Can you see the contradiction? He was a son of honour but blind and begging at the roadside.

You may want to ask, "what was the offence of Bartimaeus?" Why was he crushed so much in every way?

Well, you can find the answer in my homily last week. We are not here today to pity the biblical Bartimaeus, we have other "Spiritual Bartimaeus'" around us who deserve our pity.

Who are the spiritual Bartimaeus'?

- Bartimaeus is any man or woman who lives in a world of darkness. A world of darkness is the world occupied by anyone who doesn't know the living God. Tell them the beauty of faith in God, the power in the Eucharist, the efficacy of the rosary, or read Psalm 23 to them, give them the Bible to read, and they do not understand. They know nothing about the glories of the Lord and the joy of serving God. Some are in the Church but are blind to spiritual things. These are the Bartimaeus' you should pity.
- Bartimaeus was poor financially but rich in faith. The greatest poverty in this world is not to know or have a lively relationship with God. One may be a kind mother, a brilliant scientist, a wonderful

musician, a creative artist, a successful bank manager, a celebrated Doctor or teacher, but without having a relationship with God, such a person is so poor and wretched like the Church in Laodicea (Revelation 3:17).

- Just as Bartimaeus was at the roadside of a cursed city, many people today are living on the roadside. Take note, important activities and decisive meetings take place in the city, not the roadside. In the same way, the House of God is where the most important activity takes place; where God and humans have an encounter. This is where faith is nurtured, and hope restored. To prefer clubs, golf courses, hubs, or cinemas to Church, is to live at the roadside of life.

II. *The Grace of Bartimaeus*

Bartimaeus may have been physically blind but he was not stupid; he could think and reason well, and he had more faith than many of those around Jesus. He was shouting, *Jesus, Son of David, pity me.*

At that time, people only knew Jesus as the Son of Joseph, but Bartimaeus knew beyond this. He could not see but he recognised in his Spirit that Jesus was the promised Messiah, and that when He came, according to today's First Reading, there would be a universal restoration and the blind and lame would be part of this.

Dear friends, as I said, let us not pity Bartimaeus today; it is better to be blind and see the truth in our hearts, than to have eyes and see nothing.

People even tried to shout Bartimaeus down, but he was desperate enough not to allow the crowd to discourage him or deprive him of this opportunity.

I want to tell us something today, each time you knock on the gate of mercy, they hear it in hell and the devil uses every means to discourage us.

Maybe the reason why some of us have not received our blessings is because we are not desperate enough. Maybe we have allowed people to shout us down and tell us to stop straining our nerves in prayers and here we are; we have been suppressed in spirit. It is time to shout again and let no one stop us until God responds to us.

When the opposition is strongest, that is when we are closest to our miracle. If Bartimaeus had allowed himself to be suppressed that day, he might never have been cured. His cure was the last healing miracle of Jesus before His death.

The persistent cry of Bartimaeus attracted Jesus who waited for him. The Second Reading says we have a high priest who can sympathise with us. God always listens to the persistent cry of faith from His children. We do not serve a God who is insensitive to our plight.

When Jesus called Bartimaeus, he didn't delay; he jumped up, he threw away his identity as a beggar. Inside the cloak was the money he had made, and I imagine he must have made big money that day, as many religious visitors were around for the feast of the Passover. He left his cloak with his money, he left the mat, which was his begging apparatus, he left his location which was his begging office, and he followed in faith the voice that called him.

He didn't even think "what if he doesn't cure me?" Bartimaeus knew that once he got to Jesus, he wouldn't need his cloak, coins and office again. It is called living faith.

Many of us have been shouting for mercy too and Jesus has been calling us to come but we could not leave our cloaks, our mats, our space. What are these? These are our bitterness, unforgiveness, our sinful relationships, our passion for revenge, our attraction to sin, and as long as we hold onto them, we remain in the same space, and we can't move to Jesus.

Let me skip other details and end the story. Jesus told Bartimaeus, *Go, your faith has saved you.* I told us not to pity Bartimaeus; if we have a lively faith like Bartimaeus, we are not poor or miserable. There is nothing we can't receive from God.

Faith is the greatest currency in the divine economy. Jesus told Bartimaeus to go but he never went, he followed Jesus. Divine blessing is to call us to discipleship. When many of us receive what we want from God, we allow those things to become our excuse for going away. By following Jesus, Bartimaeus perfected his name and crowned his miracle; he became a son of honour again. There is no honour greater than becoming a disciple of Jesus.

This is Bartimaeus' story; this is the story of faith leading to restoration. This can be our story too.

Repeat this prayer after me:

Lord Jesus, give me a lively faith like Bartimaeus. Open the eyes of our minds that we may see, know and follow you. Amen.

*****

SPIRITUALITY WITHOUT CHARITY

READING TEXTS:
DEUTERONOMY 6:2-6;
PSALM 18, HEBREWS 7:23-28,
MARK 12:28-34

There are some things we often get wrong as Christians today. This morning I will just state three areas that God is calling us to re-examine and I will preach on the third point.

I. *Discipleship without Witness:*

The essence of discipleship is to become witnesses (Mark 3:14). We are not just called to pray, listen to God's Word and relax. We are sent out, to witness in the world, to Jesus. Every Christian is a missionary but very often, we miss countless opportunities to spread our faith. We are often not passionate about sharing our faith and spreading the message.

II. *The spirituality of comfort and convenience:*

We want a simple and convenient spirituality; no kneeling, no long prayers, optional or reduced rosary, and so on. We just want "something light"; a spirituality which enables us to pick and choose what we want to believe, and we drop the contents of the Christian faith that are discomforting. We want a package of spirituality that doesn't include the cross, suffering, persecutions or tribulations. This is not the version that can get one to heaven. Revelation 7:14 tells us what the Saints in heaven went through.

III. Spirituality Without Charity:

This is what I will be preaching on today, based on today's reading. The First Reading of today tells us that for own good, we must keep God's commandments and laws.

In the Gospel, Jesus tells us that the whole commandments of God rest on the foundation of love. We must love God totally and love our neighbours as God loves us. This is one of the greatest problems with the spirituality we practice today.

It's not as if we are not praying enough; we are praying, we have so many devotions and novena already. The problem is that there is not enough love in our hearts. We pray and yet we hate, criticise and judge unfairly. We are intolerant of others, we look down on people, we shun them and pay no attention to their cry for help.

You may argue that we love. Yes, we all love, but I will identify three problems with our love.

- *We love insufficiently:*
  We love but it's not enough. Love remains an abstract emotion if it doesn't move us to act on

behalf of the person we love. Jesus loves us and He died for us. We have love but it doesn't prompt us to act. We show concerns but we do not want to stain our shirts to help the one in need; like the priest and Levite in the parable of the Good Samaritan (Luke 10:25-37). We have not learnt to love sacrificially.

- *We love conditionally:*
  This is natural love. We love those who are kind to us. We love people as far as they agree with us, as far as they make sense and are obedient or useful to us. Our love doesn't include those who differ from us. This is not Christian love (Romans 5:8). The uniqueness of Christian love is that it is not con-quered or weakened by hatred; rather, it conquers hatred.

- *We love parochially:*
  We love those from our group, members of our societies, those from our race. Some of us don't like people of other nationalities; we don't like Indians or Africans; some Africans don't like Polish. Sri Lankans don't like Goans, and Goans don't like Keralans. We build all forms of strong walls and divisions on the spot where Jesus had broken down the former walls separating people (Ephesians 2:14).

Dear friends, the Lord is calling us again today to love as we are loved (Ephesians 5:2).

When we love sacrificially, unconditionally and univer-sally:

- We are fulfilling all the commandments.
- We are witnessing in the world already (love of those undeserving of love is the greatest witness).

- We are fulfilling a fundamental condition for heaven.
- We resemble God more. Love and mercy are His greatest attributes.
- We are renewing the face of the earth.

Lord Jesus teach us to love as you loved us. Use us to spread the message of your love and to renew the face of our society.
Amen.

*****

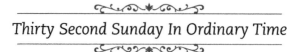

Thirty Second Sunday In Ordinary Time

THE WIDOW AND HER RICH LITTLE OFFERING

> **READING TEXTS:**
> 1 KINGS 17:10-16;
> PSALM 146; HEBREWS 9:24-28;
> MARK 12:38-44

Today is the Thirty Second Sunday in Ordinary Time, year B. I want to ask two questions before I delve into today's reflection.

- Assuming as a mother, you have only one daughter and the daughter tells you after she has graduated from university that she wants to be a Reverend Sister, would you allow her? *(The widow's offering)*

- If Jesus were to be here looking at what you would put in the offering bag, would you still put the amount you had in mind when you left the house? *(Jesus beside every collection bag/box)*

Keep these two questions in mind as we reflect on the readings of today.

The First Reading talks about the sacrifice and generosity of a widow to Elijah and the blessings she received.

The Second Reading talks about the supreme and definitive sacrifice/self-offering of Jesus.

The Gospel narrates the story of a widow who gave all she had to God; a widow who gave not just money, but a sacrifice.

All three readings point to sacrifice and generosity, but today I want to explore a different message therein.

Today, I want us to reflect on three things;

- Do not be quick to judge others.
- Do not be too quick to judge yourself.
- Do not let people's opinions and judgement control your life.

I.   *Do not be too quick to judge others.*

The widow in today's First Reading could have judged Elijah as being self-centred and greedy, insensitive and difficult. However, she would have been wrong.

The disciples of Jesus and other onlookers would have judged today's widow as being a miser and shameless. How can she drop two lepta (small coins)?

See how human judgement is different from Divine judgement. Jesus saw differently; He saw not just the gifts but the heart of the giver. Jesus watched not "what" they gave, but "how" they gave it. He was observing not what they dropped, but the attitude of the soul and the spirit with which they gave. He at once saw her condition; a woman in danger of imminent starvation (*ptochos,* translated loosely as poor). Jesus saw her huge debts and the responsibilities on her shoulders. People might have called her a shameless and stingy woman, although when she was placed on the eternal scales, her offerings weighed more than all the money in the treasury that day.

Dear friends, severally the Holy Bible warns us against hasty judgement. We are always very quick to judge people, to interpret their actions and motives and write people off as useless and tag them with all forms of unpleasant descriptions. The judgement of Jesus on the seemingly pious scribes and the seemingly shameless widow should teach us a good lesson.

We must refrain from hasty judgement because:

- Our knowledge is limited and fallible. Only God sees what we do not see. We are often wrong about people. 1 Samuel 16:7 says, ... for the Lord does not see as mortals see; they look on the outward appearance, but the Lord looks on the heart. (Also read Luke 6:37).
- To judge someone wrongly is a sin against charity and the Bible says there will be judgement without mercy for those who have not been merciful themselves (James 2:13).
- We must be careful how we judge people's actions today because, by tomorrow, we may also become victims of what we judge today (Romans 2:1-3, 1 Corinthians 10:12).

II. *Do not judge yourselves too harshly.*

Sometimes our situations are really not pleasant. We may find ourselves in misery; we may be battling with a particular weakness, we may not have what we desire immediately, our mates may seem more privileged than us, we may be at some kind of disadvantage. The two widows today are cases in point. They could have been "bitter" with themselves.

My simple message for us is that we should stop over analysing our problems; stop our bitter and nagging feeling; step down from the feeling of anger and insecurity. We are not a finished product. Work is still in progress on us, so we should be at peace with ourselves and focus on what God has done and could do with us.

III. *Do not allow people's judgement and opinion to ruin you.*

If the widow had considered what people would say, she wouldn't have stepped forward, but she did. She assured herself that in the long run, it was between her and her God.

One of the things we should not allow to control our lives and destinies, is people's unfair judgements and opinions about us. This is what the devil uses most to weigh us down, sometimes to give us false confidence that we are doing well and most often to discourage us from the good we intend, or we have started. Always keep in mind that after all, the most important judgement is what God sees and says about us.

People may not believe in us, people may give up on us, people may misinterpret us, and say all kinds of calumny against us. People might have concluded on us, but we should not stop believing in ourselves. Do not stop believing in God, and do not ever lose faith and hope. God sees what everyone doesn't see. He sees most especially our struggles and good intentions.

*****

WHEN ALL SHALL END

READING TEXTS:
DANIEL 12:1-3;
PSALM 16, HEBREWS 10:11-14, 18;
MARK 13:24-32

Today is the Thirty Third Sunday in Ordinary Time, year B and next Sunday will be the solemnity of Christ the King. With that celebration, we shall end the last Sunday in year B and begin a new liturgical season and year.

As the liturgical year runs to an end and also as we approach the end of the calendar year, the Church directs our minds to focus on the fact that whatever has a beginning must have an end, be that human life, our earthly existence, this world, or our experiences, sweet or bitter.

Many of us don't like to think of the end of life. Many of us don't even believe that the world will end one day (we have defined our truth), and many more are struggling to understand how it will end; maybe by ecological damage, by a nuclear weapon, universal inferno or flood?

"How" is left to God but human life and the physical world will one day come to an end.

Let us reflect on the readings of today. The First Reading of today is the vision revealed to Daniel about the end of human existence. They contain truths that some of us may not like to hear.

Five things are worthy of note.

- The dead will all rise again as earthly existence is not all there is. There is life after death. Jesus re-confirmed this in John 5:28.
- They will be judged according to how they had lived. Which means we must all render an account of our lives, even those who believe they are not responsible to anyone.
  (Romans 14:12, 2 Corinthians 5:10).
- A book of life shall be opened which means the record is being kept about us.
  (Read Tobith 12:12-13).
- Anyone whose name is not found there shall go to everlasting shame. John re-confirmed that this is true (Revelation 20:11-15; also, John 5:29).
- Those whose names are found will enjoy everlasting life and they will shine as brightly as the vault of heaven and bright as stars for all eternity.

The Psalm of today calls it the fullness of joy, happiness forever. Who are those who will go to this everlasting life of joy and happiness? Daniel described them as, *the learned /wise and those who have instructed others in virtue.*

Who are these?

I. *The wise/learned:*

The wise are those who fear the Lord and walk in His ways. The world may think they are foolish, religious, anachronistic and simple, but they are the wisest. Proverbs 9:10 *To fear the Lord is the beginning of wisdom, and to acknowledge the Holy One is understanding.* (Also read Malachi 3:16-18).

II. *Those who have instructed others in virtue:*

These are those who by word and example have tried to bring others to love and appreciate the Christian faith; parents who teach their children to know and love God, wives who convert their husbands and vice versa, a friend who brings another friend to Jesus.

Do we have a problem with any of these truths? That human life will end one day? That Jesus will come again? That the dead will rise again? That they will be judged? That some will go to everlasting shame?

Well, this is what we profess every Sunday when we recite the Creed. This is what Jesus Himself taught us as recorded in the Scriptures.

In the Second Reading, the author tells us that Christ has offered one single sacrifice for us.

For those who are thinking there can never be hell or eternal punishment and that God will have mercy on all the dead, listen. Christ has already done His part. He has offered the sacrifice of mercy once and for all, so whoever refuses to embrace the merit has chosen damnation.

And now He sits at God's right. Doing What?

- Interceding for us, so that we don't end our lives in sorrow.
- Preparing to come again in glory to judge the living and the dead.

The Gospel contains words from the very mouth of Jesus. He described in vivid imageries His second coming and the scary events that will precede it.

Each time we talk about the end of life, the second coming, the end of the world, the final judgement, many people are scared; many people take it as a divine joke, and many are indifferent.

Well, we are mainly scared because we are not sure of ourselves; because we know within ourselves that we have failed to be faithful in our relationship with God and our duties as Christians in the world.

Otherwise, the news that Jesus will come again or that He will call us to come, should fill us with joy; the joy that we are going into glory, we are going into eternal happiness with our God and Saviour, we are going into a realm of lasting peace, we are going to be reunited with our beloved ones who have faithfully departed this world. Are we not supposed to be eager about this? Are we not supposed to wait in joyful hope for this wonderful coming?

Dear friends, let us make up our minds to be among the wise who absolutely acknowledge God as their Creator and Lord, and who worship Him faithfully and serve Him righteously. Let us be among those who will help others to come back to God. Let us pray to God to deliver us from whatever may cause us to fear the coming in glory of Jesus.

INDEX

BOOKS BY THE SAME AUTHOR

He Sent Forth His Word, Series 1: Homilies for Sundays, Year A.

He Sent Forth His Word, Series 3: Homilies for Sundays, Year C.

He Sent Forth His Word, Series 4: Homilies for the Liturgical Seasons of Advent, Christmas, Lent and Easter.

He Sent Forth His Word, Series 5: Homilies for Feasts and Solemnities.

He Sent Forth His Word, Series 6: Homilies for Weekdays, Cycle I.

He Sent Forth His Word, Series 7: Homilies for Weekdays, Cycle II.

Light to my Path: A Collection of Retreat Talks and Reflections.

His Voice goes Forth: A Collection of Vocal Meditations and Nuggets.

Lord, teach us to pray: Prayers for Various Occasions.

Seven Days Journey with the Lord: A Handbook for a Self-facilitated Retreat.

Praying with the Psalms.

What God has Joined together: A Handbook for Marriage Preparation Course.

Whom Shall I send: A Seven-day Journey with the Lord through His Word.

They Shall be Called My Children: Reflections and Prayers for Children.

When the Spirit Comes Upon You, Series 1:
A Nine-day Reflection and Prayers for the Gifts of the Holy Spirit.

When the Spirit Comes Upon You, Series 2:
A Twelve-day Reflection and Prayers for the Fruits of the Holy Spirit.

When the Spirit Comes Upon You, Series 3:
A Nine-day Reflection and Prayers for the Manifestation of the Holy Spirit.

*****

Printed in Great Britain
by Amazon

46164869R00098